75 smoothies

75 smoothies

How to make fabulous fresh fruit drinks, shakes and floats with over 290 step-by-step photographs

SUZANNAH OLIVIER

southwater

This edition is published by Southwater, an imprint of Anness Publishing Ltd
Hermes House, 88–89 Blackfriars Road, London SE1 8HA
tel. 020 7401 2077; fax 020 7633 9499; www.southwaterbooks.com; www.annesspublishing.com

If you like the images in this book and would like to investigate using them for publishing,
promotions or advertising, please visit our website www.practicalpictures.com for more information.

UK agent: The Manning Partnership Ltd; tel. 01225 478444; fax 01225 478440; sales@manningpartnership.co.uk
UK distributor: Grantham Book Services Ltd; tel. 01476 541080; fax 01476 541061; orders@gbs.tbs-ltd.co.uk
North American agent/distributor: National Book Network; tel. 301 459 3366; fax 301 429 5746; www.nbnbooks.com
Australian agent/distributor: Pan Macmillan Australia; tel. 1300 135 113; fax 1300 135 103;
customer.service@macmillan.com.au
New Zealand agent/distributor: David Bateman Ltd; tel. (09) 415 7664; fax (09) 415 8892

Publisher: Joanna Lorenz
Editors: Joy Wotton and Clare Gooden
Photographers: Gus Filgate and Craig Robertson, with
additional pictures by Janine Hosegood and Simon Smith
Stylist: Helen Trent

Designer: Nigel Partridge
Cover Designer: Balley Design Associates
Additional Recipes: Susannah Blake, Nicola Graimes
and Jane Milton
Production Controller: Wendy Lawson

ETHICAL TRADING POLICY
Because of our ongoing ecological investment programme, you, as our customer, can have the pleasure and reassurance
of knowing that a tree is being cultivated on your behalf to naturally replace the materials used to make the book you are
holding. For further information about this scheme, go to www.annesspublishing.com/trees

Previously published as part of a larger volume, *Juicing, Smoothies & Blended Drinks*

Publisher's Note: Although the advice and information in this book are believed to be accurate and true
at the time of going to press, neither the authors nor the publisher can accept any legal responsibility
or liability for any errors or omissions that may be made.

NOTES
Bracketed terms are intended for American readers.

For all recipes, quantities are given in both metric and imperial measures and, where
appropriate, measures are also given in standard cups and spoons. Follow one set,
but not a mixture, because they are not interchangeable.

Standard spoon and cup measures are level.
1 tsp = 5ml, 1 tbsp = 15ml, 1 cup = 250ml/8fl oz

Australian standard tablespoons are 20ml. Australian readers should use 3 tsp
in place of 1 tbsp for measuring small quantities.

Medium (US large) eggs are used unless otherwise stated.

The very young, elderly and those in ill-health or with a compromised immune system are advised
against consuming juices or blends that contain raw eggs.

Always check the manufacturer's instructions before using a blender
or food processor to crush ice.

CONTENTS

Introduction

Smoothies, shakes and blends have become extremely popular in recent years. They fit neatly into hectic modern lives, enabling you to incorporate healthy habits into your everyday routines. The main advantage of smoothies is that they are easy to make, quick, convenient and packed with rejuvenating, healing and revitalizing nutrients. On top of all this, they are also delicious, and a luxurious blended drink can feel like a real treat.

Health Benefits

While you can buy ready-made smoothies, nothing quite beats the taste of a blend made at home. Freshly made drinks are also a more potent source of nutrients and certain combinations have specific health benefits. If you drink fresh blends on a regular basis, you'll enjoy clearer skin, better energy levels and balanced overall health.

It is well known that the antioxidants found in fruits and vegetables work most effectively when they are consumed together, and blending encourages precisely this. Combinations of specific different ingredients can be used to emphasize particular flavours or effects in the same way that you would in cooking – sweet and sour, savoury and spicy, warming or cooling – but you can afford to be more adventurous than you might be with conventionally prepared foods. The flavours of a fruit or vegetable often taste much better

Above: Fresh flavours are whizzed up into nutrient-packed blends in minutes.

than when the produce is cooked or even served raw. For instance, you may not particularly like prunes when served stewed, but blend them with apple and orange and you get a completely different, more complex and utterly delicious taste sensation.

Drink Yourself Well

Even if you feel like going off the rails and indulging in extra ingredients, such as chocolate, alcohol or coffee, the very fact that the smoothie is based on fresh fruits and vegetables means that you are still getting a wonderful boost of vitamins, antioxidants and minerals.

Preparing smoothies and blends also has an excellent psychological benefit. Just making a smoothie can make you feel good – you will feel you are nurturing and pampering yourself – and in addition, by using lots of fresh natural ingredients you will boost your own health and the health of your family.

Left: Let children get involved in blending and watch them reap the benefits.

Above: Blenders and food processors will turn soft fruits into the most delicious smoothies and milkshakes.

A Brief History of Smoothies

The healing power of certain foods was recognized by Hippocrates who said "Let food be your medicine." Since time immemorial, food, water and healing herbs have been the cornerstones of the healing arts.

Below: The process of making blended drinks is as enjoyable as drinking them.

In the 19th century, doctors and naturopaths were using fresh fruit and vegetable blends and juices to improve the health of their patients. Many well-known pioneers were responsible for major discoveries about the therapeutic properties of blends and juices. People such as Dr Kellogg, Father Kniepp, Dr Max Bircher-Bener and Dr Max Gerson all helped to popularize the notion of the "juice cure".

The Natural Way to Health

In our modern, fast-paced lives, health drinks provide easy-to-make snacks, quick breakfasts and fast energy boosters. The introduction of advanced kitchen technology, such as blenders, food processors and juicers, has made the preparation of blends and juices swift and easy. They are a convenient way of achieving the target of five portions of fruit and vegetables a day.

In addition to their more general health-boosting properties, smoothies and blends are also used for specific cleansing and detoxing, for helping speed recovery from illness and as part of anti-ageing regimes. A school of thought maintains that blends can help prevent some cancers, although this has yet to be proven. Nevertheless, freshly made

Above: Raw ingredients that can be included in smoothies provide all the vitamins and minerals you need.

fruit and vegetable smoothies and blends provide many of the essential vitamins and minerals that are vital for a long and healthy life.

Smoothies are fun to make and to share: invent fruit-filled concoctions, or skip the coffee and share a fruit-packed blend or a smoothie with a friend. How wonderful that something so healthy should also taste so good.

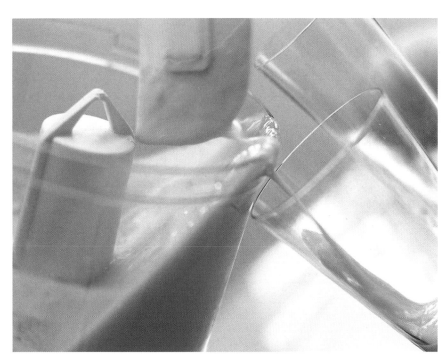

BLENDERS ARE BEST

Smoothies made in a blender are different from juices made in a juicer in one important way: they retain the fibre of the fruits. Fibre is not only important for healthy digestion, but also for cardiovascular health, and for helping balance blood-sugar levels. When choosing equipment, bear in mind that fibre is valuable in the diet and, while juicing will not replace eating whole fruits and vegetables, smoothies and other blended drinks are nutritionally equivalent to eating the whole fruit. However, nutritional guidelines state that one glass of juice does count towards the recommended total daily intake of five portions of fruit and vegetables.

easy
breakfast
blends

Breakfast is the most important meal of the day, but also the most neglected, so give yourself a kick-start with these fuel-packed, imaginative drinks. Made in minutes and easier to digest than a bowl of cereal, fabulous fresh fruit blends and decadent smoothies provide the perfect early-morning boost.

Creamy banana boost

Bananas are a great energy food. They are packed with valuable nutrients and healthy carbohydrates, and they also fill you up – which is definitely a bonus. Blended with the additional fruits – pineapple, dates and lemon juice – and creamy milk, this delicious concoction will keep you going for hours. If you're prone to snacking throughout the day, try this and you'll feel all the better for it. Any leftover drink can be stored in the refrigerator for up to a day.

Makes 2–3 tall glasses

½ pineapple
4 Medjool dates, pitted
1 small ripe banana
juice of 1 lemon
300ml/½ pint/1¼ cups very cold full cream (whole) milk or soya milk

Cook's tip
The Medjool date is considered to be the jewel of all dates because of its size, texture and sweetness. It originates from Morocco, where it was reserved for royal hosts and other dignitaries centuries ago. Nowadays we can all enjoy them.

1 Using a small, sharp knife, cut away the skin and core from the pineapple. Roughly chop the flesh and put it in a blender or food processor, then add the pitted dates.

2 Peel and chop the banana and add it to the rest of the fruit together with the lemon juice.

3 Blend thoroughly until smooth, stopping to scrape the mixture down from the side of the bowl with a rubber spatula, if necessary.

4 Add the milk to the blender or food processor and process until well combined. Pour the smoothie into tall glasses and serve immediately.

Zesty soya smoothie

Whizzed up with freshly squeezed orange juice, a splash of tangy lemon and a little fragrant honey, tofu can be transformed into a drink that's smooth, creamy, nutritious and delicious. Most people would not think to add tofu to a blended drink, but please do try it – you will be genuinely surprised. If possible, try to get hold of some silken tofu for this smoothie, as it has a wonderful satiny texture that blends particularly well.

Makes 1 large glass

2 oranges
15ml/1 tbsp lemon juice
20–25ml/4–5 tsp sunflower honey or herb honey
150g/5oz tofu
long, thin strips of pared orange rind, to decorate

Cook's tip
For a smooth drink, strain the liquid through a sieve (strainer) after blending to remove the orange rind.

1 Finely grate the rind of one orange and set aside. Use a citrus juicer to juice both oranges and pour the juice into a food processor or blender. Add the grated orange rind, lemon juice, sunflower or herb honey and tofu.

2 Blend the ingredients until smooth and creamy, then pour into a glass. Decorate with the pared orange rind and serve.

Opposite: Creamy banana boost (left) and Zesty soya smoothie (right)

Creamy banana boost Energy 187kcal/793kJ; Protein 4.7g; Carbohydrate 34.6g, of which sugars 34g; Fat 4.3g, of which saturates 2.5g; Cholesterol 14mg; Calcium 152mg; Fibre 2.5g; Sodium 48mg.
Zesty soya smoothie Energy 350kcal/1483kJ; Protein 15.6g; Carbohydrate 60.9g, of which sugars 60.3g; Fat 6.6g, of which saturates 0.8g; Cholesterol 0mg; Calcium 908mg; Fibre 5.1g; Sodium 26mg .

Dairy-free deluxe

Prunes, apples, oranges and soya milk may seem like an unusual combination but the results are absolutely fabulous. Sweet, caramel-rich and very drinkable, this is a great milkshake for both adults and children, and, of course, for anyone on a dairy-free diet. Regular cow's milk can be used, if you prefer, but if you are watching the calories, use skimmed milk. The resulting drink will not be quite as creamy, but it will still be delicious.

Makes 1 tall glass

2 small eating apples
5 ready-to-eat pitted prunes
juice of 1 orange
60ml/4 tbsp soya milk
ice cubes

Cook's tip
Any eating apples can be used for this drink. Select different types of apples depending on whether you prefer a tart flavour or a sweet. Try pears for a different variation.

1 Using a small, sharp knife, remove the core from the apples and chop into chunks – but do not peel them. Push half the chopped apple through a juicer, followed by the prunes and the remaining chopped apple.

2 Pour the apple and prune juice into a jug (pitcher) and add the orange juice and soya milk. Whisk lightly until smooth and frothy. Pour into a chunky glass and serve immediately, adding a few cubes of ice.

Pear flair

For a truly refreshing combination, you can't do much better than a mixture of juicy pears and grapes. Wheatgerm adds body for a sustained energy fix and soya yogurt turns the juice into a protein-packed milkshake with a lusciously light and frothy topping. This really is quite a filling drink and is a great choice for those who feel that their life is too busy to prepare really nutritious food. A quick and easy drink that is good for you too – what could be better?

Makes 1 large glass

1 large pear
150g/5oz/1¼ cups green grapes
15ml/1 tbsp wheatgerm
60ml/4 tbsp soya yogurt
ice cubes

Cook's tip
If you would prefer to use a dairy yogurt rather than the soya variety, substitute with the type of your choice. It is better that you stick with a natural (plain) yogurt as plenty of fruity flavour is gained from the pear and the grapes. Look for the 0 per cent fat varieties.

1 Using a vegetable peeler, peel the pear and chop the flesh into large chunks of roughly the same size. Seed the grapes if necessary.

2 Push half the pear chunks through a juicer, followed by the grapes and then the remaining chunks of pear. Transfer the juice to a small jug (pitcher).

3 Add the wheatgerm to the yogurt and stir to mix thoroughly.

4 Pour into the pear and grape juice, whisking until it is light and frothy. Pour the milkshake over ice cubes and serve.

Opposite: Dairy-free deluxe (left) and Pear flair (right)

Dairy-free deluxe Energy 248kcal/1059kJ; Protein 5.1g; Carbohydrate 56.7g, of which sugars 56.7g; Fat 1.6g, of which saturates 0.2g; Cholesterol 0mg; Calcium 55mg; Fibre 9g; Sodium 39mg.
Pear flair Energy 247kcal/1048kJ; Protein 8.1g; Carbohydrate 47.1g, of which sugars 42.8g; Fat 2.8g, of which saturates 0.6g; Cholesterol 1mg; Calcium 44mg; Fibre 6.7g; Sodium 8mg.

Orange and raspberry smoothie

This exquisite blend combines the sharp-sweet taste of raspberries and the refreshing fruitiness of oranges with smooth yogurt. It tastes like creamy fruit heaven in a glass. Even better, it takes just minutes to prepare, making it perfect as a quick breakfast juice for people in a hurry or, indeed, as a refreshing drink at any other time of day.

1 Place the raspberries and yogurt in a blender or food processor and process for about 1 minute until the mixture is smooth and creamy.

2 Add the orange juice to the raspberry and yogurt mixture and process for another 30 seconds or until thoroughly combined. Pour into tall glasses and serve immediately.

Makes 2–3 glasses

250g/9oz/1⅓ cups raspberries, chilled
200ml/7fl oz/scant 1 cup natural (plain) yogurt, chilled
300ml/½ pint/1¼ cups freshly squeezed orange juice, chilled

Cook's tip
For a super-chilled version, use frozen raspberries instead of fresh. You may need to blend the raspberries and yogurt for a little longer to get a really smooth result.

Orange and raspberry smoothie Energy 94kcal/401kJ; Protein 5.1g; Carbohydrate 17.6g, of which sugars 17.6g; Fat 1g, of which saturates 0.4g; Cholesterol 1mg; Calcium 158mg; Fibre 2.2g; Sodium 68mg.

Mango and lime lassi

Inspired by the classic Indian drink, this tangy, fruity blend is great for breakfast or as a delicious pick-me-up at any time of day. Soft, ripe mango blended with yogurt and sharp, zesty lime and lemon juice makes a wonderfully thick, cooling drink that's packed with energy. It can also be enjoyed as a mellow soother when you need to unwind.

Makes 2 tall glasses

1 mango
finely grated rind and juice of 1 lime
15ml/1 tbsp lemon juice
5–10ml/1–2 tsp caster (superfine) sugar
100ml/3½fl oz/scant ½ cup natural
   (plain) yogurt
mineral water
1 extra lime, halved, to serve

1 Peel the mango and cut the flesh from the stone (pit). Put the flesh into a blender or food processor and add the lime rind and juice.

2 Add the lemon juice, sugar and natural yogurt. Whizz until completely smooth, scraping down the sides of the bowl, if necessary. Stir in a little mineral water to thin it down.

3 Serve immediately, with half a lime on the side of each glass so that more juice can be squeezed in, if desired.

Mango and lime lassi Energy 81kcal/344kJ; Protein 3.1g; Carbohydrate 17g, of which sugars 16.7g; Fat 0.7g, of which saturates 0.4g; Cholesterol 1mg; Calcium 106mg; Fibre 2g; Sodium 43mg.

Sweet dream

A soothing blend guaranteed to wake you up slowly, this fruity threesome is naturally sweet so there is no need for any additional sugar. Fresh grapefruit juice marries brilliantly with the dried fruits, and rich creamy yogurt makes a delicious contrast of colour and flavour – simply perfect to sip over a leisurely breakfast while reading the newspaper.

Makes 2 glasses

25g/1oz/scant ¼ cup dried figs or
   dates, stoned (pitted)
50g/2oz/¼ cup ready-to-eat prunes
25g/1oz/scant ¼ cup sultanas (golden raisins)
1 grapefruit
350ml/12fl oz/1½ cups full cream
   (whole) milk
30ml/2 tbsp Greek (US strained plain) yogurt

Cook's tip
For a dairy-free version of this drink, use soya yogurt and soya or rice milk instead of ordinary milk. The consistency of the smoothie will not be as creamy but it will still be delicious – and perhaps better for those who prefer a lighter drink.

1 Put the dried fruits in a blender or food processor. Squeeze the grapefruit juice and add to the machine. Blend until smooth, scraping the mixture down from the side of the bowl, if necessary. Add the milk and blend until completely smooth.

2 Using a teaspoon, tap a spoonful of the yogurt around the inside of each of two tall glasses. Pour in the fruit mixture and serve immediately.

Sweet dream Energy 246kcal/1033kJ; Protein 8.6g; Carbohydrate 38.3g, of which sugars 38.3g; Fat 7.4g, of which saturates 4.5g; Cholesterol 25mg; Calcium 301mg; Fibre 3.7g; Sodium 103mg.

Raspberry and oatmeal smoothie

Just a spoonful or so of oatmeal gives substance to this tangy, invigorating drink. If you can, prepare it ahead of time because soaking the raw oats helps to break down the starch into natural sugars that are easy to digest. The smoothie will thicken up in the refrigerator so you might need to stir in a little extra juice or mineral water just before serving.

Makes 1 large glass

25ml/1½ tbsp medium oatmeal
150g/5oz/scant 1 cup raspberries
5–10ml/1–2 tsp clear honey
45ml/3 tbsp natural (plain) yogurt

1 Spoon the oatmeal into a heatproof bowl. Pour in 120ml/4fl oz/½ cup boiling water and leave to stand for about 10 minutes.

2 Put the soaked oats in a blender or food processor and add all but two or three of the raspberries, the honey and about 30ml/2 tbsp of the yogurt. Process until smooth, scraping down the side of the bowl if necessary.

Cook's tip
If you don't like raspberry pips (seeds) in your smoothies, press the fruit through a sieve (strainer) with the back of a wooden spoon to make a smooth purée, then process with the oatmeal and yogurt as before. Alternatively, try using redcurrants instead of the raspberries.

Although a steaming bowl of porridge can't be beaten as a winter warmer, this smooth, oaty drink makes a great, light alternative in warmer months. It is a good way to make sure you get your fill of wholesome oats for breakfast.

3 Pour the raspberry and oatmeal smoothie into a large glass, swirl in the remaining yogurt and top with the reserved raspberries.

Raspberry and oatmeal smoothie Energy 171kcal/728kJ; Protein 7.2g; Carbohydrate 31.1g, of which sugars 12.9g; Fat 3g, of which saturates 0.3g; Cholesterol 1mg; Calcium 131mg; Fibre 4.8g; Sodium 50mg.

Muesli smoothly

Another great breakfast booster, this store-cupboard smoothie can be a lifesaver if you've run out of fresh fruit. It's also a perfect option for breakfast in bed without the crumbs. Any extra drink can be covered and stored overnight in the refrigerator, although you'll probably need to add more milk in the morning as it will undoubtedly thicken on standing.

Makes 2 glasses

1 piece preserved stem ginger, plus
   30ml/2 tbsp syrup from the ginger jar
50g/2oz/¼ cup ready-to-eat dried apricots,
   halved or quartered
40g/1½oz/scant ½ cup natural
   muesli (granola)
about 200ml/7fl oz/scant 1 cup
   semi-skimmed (low-fat) milk

Cook's tip
Apricot and ginger are perfect partners in this divine drink. It makes an incredibly healthy, tasty breakfast, but is so delicious and indulgent that you could even serve it as a dessert after a summer meal.

1 Chop the preserved ginger and put it in a blender or food processor with the syrup, apricots, muesli and milk.

2 Process until smooth, adding more milk if necessary. Serve in wide glasses.

Muesli smoothly Energy 203kcal/862kJ; Protein 6.4g; Carbohydrate 40.1g, of which sugars 30.9g; Fat 3.2g, of which saturates 1.3g; Cholesterol 6mg; Calcium 163mg; Fibre 2.9g; Sodium 163mg.

Big breakfast

Easy to prepare and even easier to drink, this energy-packed smoothie makes a great start to the day. Bananas and sesame seeds provide the perfect fuel in the form of slow-release carbohydrate that will keep you going all morning, while fresh and zesty orange juice and sweet, scented mango will set your tastebuds tingling first thing.

Makes 2 glasses

½ mango
1 banana
1 large orange
30ml/2 tbsp wheat bran
15ml/1 tbsp sesame seeds
10–15ml/2–3 tsp honey

Cook's tip
Mango juice is naturally very sweet so you may wish to add less honey or leave it out altogether. Taste the drink to decide how much you need.

1 Using a small, sharp knife, skin the mango, then slice the flesh off the stone (pit). Peel the banana and break it into short lengths, then place it in a blender or food processor with the mango.

2 Squeeze the juice from the orange and add to the blender or food processor along with the bran, sesame seeds and honey. Whizz until the mixture is smooth and creamy, then pour into glasses and serve.

Big breakfast Energy 123kcal/523kJ; Protein 3.4g; Carbohydrate 26.9g, of which sugars 23.7g; Fat 1g, of which saturates 0.2g; Cholesterol 0mg; Calcium 40mg; Fibre 3.6g; Sodium 5mg.

Late breakfast

This energizing blend is simply bursting with goodness, just what you need when the morning has got off to a slow start. Not only is tofu a perfect source of protein, it is also rich in minerals and contains nutrients that help strengthen the immune system. Blended with seeds and vitamin-rich strawberries, this creamy blend should see you through until lunchtime. Store any leftovers in the refrigerator for later in the day or the following morning.

Makes 2 glasses

250g/9oz firm tofu
200g/7oz/1¾ cups strawberries
45ml/3 tbsp pumpkin or sunflower seeds, plus extra for sprinkling
30–45ml/2–3 tbsp clear honey
juice of 2 large oranges
juice of 1 lemon

Cook's tip
Almost any other fruit can be used instead of the strawberries. Those that blend well, such as mangoes, bananas, peaches, plums and raspberries, work particularly well as a substitute.

1 Roughly chop the tofu, then hull and roughly chop the strawberries. Reserve a few strawberry chunks.

2 Put all the ingredients in a blender or food processor and blend until completely smooth, scraping the mixture down from the side of the bowl, if necessary.

3 Pour into tumblers and sprinkle with extra seeds and strawberry chunks.

Late breakfast Energy 310kcal/1296kJ; Protein 15.7g; Carbohydrate 26.9g, of which sugars 22.6g; Fat 16.1g, of which saturates 1.7g; Cholesterol 0mg; Calcium 684mg; Fibre 2.5g; Sodium 19mg.

A good fix

While some people thrive on a glass of freshly juiced fruits first thing in the morning, others can't quite get going without their daily caffeine fix in the form of strong coffee. This gorgeous mocha smoothie combines decadent dark chocolate and caffeine-rich coffee in a deliciously frothy energizing mix that is packed with calcium. This is an intensely sweet and indulgent way to start the day – so don't treat yourself too often.

Makes 1 large glass

40g/1½oz plain (semisweet) chocolate, plus extra for decoration
5–10ml/1–2 tsp instant espresso powder
300ml/½ pint/1¼ cups full cream (whole) milk
30ml/2 tbsp double (heavy) cream (optional)
ice cubes
cocoa powder (unsweetened), for dusting

1 Chop the chocolate into pieces and place in a small, heavy pan with the espresso powder and 100ml/3½fl oz/ scant ½ cup of the milk. Heat very gently, stirring with a wooden spoon, until the chocolate has melted. Remove from the heat and pour into a bowl. Leave to cool for 10 minutes.

2 Add the remaining milk and cream, if using, and whisk the mixture together until smooth and frothy – you could use a handheld blender wand. Pour the smoothie over ice cubes in a large glass or mug and serve sprinkled with cocoa powder and chocolate shavings.

A good fix Energy 402kcal/1677kJ; Protein 11.9g; Carbohydrate 38.9g, of which sugars 38.5g; Fat 22.9g, of which saturates 14.2g; Cholesterol 44mg; Calcium 367mg; Fibre 1g; Sodium 131mg.

smooth
and
simple

Refreshingly tangy or as smooth as silk, super
smoothies have earned their place as one of our
favourite drinks. Keep them simple with pure fruit
blends, or try something a little different by adding
creamed coconut, fruit tea, herbs or spices.
Let the ideas in this irresistible chapter inspire you
to experiment with all kinds of combinations.

Berry smooth

This simple recipe uses oat milk, a cholesterol-free, calcium-rich alternative to cow's milk, and a good partner to sweet summer fruits. Although a good store-cupboard stand-by, you might prefer to keep the oat milk in the refrigerator, ready for an impromptu milkshake whenever you're in the mood. For a really chilled, extremely refreshing flavour, use a mixed bag of semi-thawed frozen fruits, which will blend to a fabulously thick consistency.

Makes 2 glasses

250g/9oz frozen mixed summer fruits, partially thawed, plus extra to garnish
130g/4½oz/generous ½ cup soya yogurt
45ml/3 tbsp vanilla syrup
350ml/12fl oz/1½ cups oat milk

Cook's tip
Vanilla syrup is really sweet and full of flavour, great for giving drinks and desserts a deep, mellow aroma. If you cannot find any, use 45ml/3 tbsp caster (superfine) sugar and 5ml/1 tsp good quality vanilla extract.

1 Put the partially thawed mixed summer fruits in a blender or food processor. Add the soya yogurt and blend thoroughly to make a thick purée. Scrape the mixture down from the side of the bowl with a rubber spatula, if necessary, and blend again, briefly, to incorporate into the mixture.

2 Add the vanilla syrup and oat milk to the fruit purée and blend the mixture again until smooth.

3 Transfer the smoothie to a small jug (pitcher) and chill, or pour it into two tall glasses and serve immediately, decorated with the extra fruits.

Pear, rhubarb and cranberry cooler

For best results this delicious smoothie should be made with really ripe and extremely juicy pears, so if the ones you buy are hard, leave them in the fruit bowl for several days before making this fresh and fruity treat. Do not forget to cook the rhubarb well in advance so that it has plenty of time to cool down before you start blending.

Makes 3–4 glasses

400g/14oz early rhubarb
2 large ripe pears
130g/4½oz/generous 1 cup fresh or frozen cranberries
90g/3½oz/½ cup caster (superfine) sugar
mineral water (optional)

Cook's tip
If you are using frozen cranberries, don't bother to thaw them first. They'll still blend, and their icy coolness will chill the smoothie to just the right temperature.

1 Using a small, sharp knife, trim the rhubarb and cut into 2cm/¾in lengths.

2 Place the rhubarb slices in a pan with 90ml/6 tbsp water and cover with a tight-fitting lid. Cook gently for about 5 minutes or until tender. Transfer to a bowl and leave to cool, putting several pieces aside for garnish.

3 Peel, quarter and core the pears and put into a blender or food processor with the cranberries, the rhubarb and its cooking juices and the sugar.

4 Blend until smooth, scraping down the side of the bowl, if necessary. Thin with mineral water, if you like, then serve, garnished with the rhubarb pieces.

Berry smooth Energy 204kcal/856kJ; Protein 9.4g; Carbohydrate 29.2g, of which sugars 29.2g; Fat 4.1g, of which saturates 0.9g; Cholesterol 1mg; Calcium 47mg; Fibre 1.4g; Sodium 125mg.
Pear, rhubarb and cranberry cooler Energy 138kcal/590kJ; Protein 1.4g; Carbohydrate 34.9g, of which sugars 34.9g; Fat 0.2g, of which saturates 0g; Cholesterol 0mg; Calcium 115mg; Fibre 3.6g; Sodium 7mg.

Ruby dreamer

Figs have a distinctive yet delicate taste and are best used in simple combinations, with ingredients that enhance, rather than mask, their flavour. Like most fruits, fresh figs are now available most of the year but they are often at their best in winter when ruby oranges are also in season – giving you the perfect excuse to make this veritable treat of a smoothie.

1 Cut off the hard, woody tips from the stalks of the figs, then use a sharp knife to cut each fruit in half.

2 Squeeze the oranges, using a citrus juicer or by hand. Pour the juice into a blender or food processor and add the figs and sugar. Process well until the mixture is really smooth and fairly thick, scraping the fruit down from the side of the bowl, if necessary.

3 Add lemon juice and blend briefly. Pour over crushed ice and serve.

Makes 2 glasses

6 large ripe figs
4 ruby oranges
15ml/1 tbsp dark muscovado (molasses) sugar
30–45ml/2–3 tbsp lemon juice
crushed ice

Cook's tip
If you cannot find ruby oranges, use any other type of orange. The colour of the juice, however, will not be quite so vibrant.

Ruby dreamer Energy 417kcal/1776kJ; Protein 7.2g; Carbohydrate 97.8g, of which sugars 97.8g; Fat 2.5g, of which saturates 0g; Cholesterol 0mg; Calcium 443mg; Fibre 13.8g; Sodium 96mg.

Rosemary nectar

This is one of those smoothies that's only worth making if you've got the perfect, ripe ingredients. The fabulously aromatic fragrance of fresh rosemary reacts with the sweet, scented flavour of juicy nectarines to produce a delicious blend with a mouthwatering taste that will almost explode on your tongue – make plenty as you're sure to want more.

Makes 3 glasses

4 long rosemary sprigs, plus extra
　to decorate
15ml/1 tbsp golden caster (superfine) sugar
2.5ml/½ tsp ground ginger
2 oranges
4 nectarines
ice cubes

1 Put the rosemary sprigs in a small pan with the sugar, ground ginger and 150ml/¼ pint/⅔ cup water. Heat gently until the sugar dissolves, then simmer for 1 minute. Remove from the heat, transfer the sprigs and syrup to a bowl and leave to cool.

2 Squeeze the oranges. Halve and stone (pit) the nectarines and put in a food processor or blender with the orange juice. Process until smooth but don't worry if there are a few specks of nectarine skin dotting the juice.

3 Remove the rosemary from the syrup and pour into the juice. Blend briefly.

4 Put a few ice cubes in each glass and fill with the juice. Serve immediately, with extra rosemary sprigs to decorate.

Cook's tip
If you've bought nectarines only to find that they're as hard as bullets, leave them in the fruit bowl for a couple of days – they should ripen fairly quickly.

Rosemary nectar Energy 123kcal/527kJ; Protein 3.5g; Carbohydrate 28.7g, of which sugars 28.7g; Fat 0.3g, of which saturates 0g; Cholesterol 0mg; Calcium 61mg; Fibre 3.7g; Sodium 7mg

Smooth and simple

Pre-packed and ready to use, a mixed bag of summer fruits (which can be bought from the freezer section in most large supermarkets) makes an unbelievably simple, fruity base for drinks. The frozen fruits mean that the final blend is perfectly chilled as well, so you don't need to add ice. Mixed with orange juice and enriched with a tempting swirl of cream, this smoothie is made in a flash – the perfect accompaniment to a relaxing afternoon in the sunshine.

Makes 3 glasses

500g/1lb 2oz frozen mixed summer fruits,
    partially thawed
30ml/2 tbsp caster (superfine) sugar
about 300ml/½ pint/1¼ cups freshly
    squeezed orange juice
60ml/4 tbsp single (light) cream

Cook's tip
If you do not want to squeeze the oranges, you can buy juice – but avoid the concentrated types.

1 Put all but a few of the summer fruits into a blender or food processor and add the sugar and orange juice. Blend until smooth, adding a little more orange juice if the mixture is too thick.

2 Pour the smoothie into 3 tall glasses and, using a teaspoon, swirl a little cream into each glass. Top with the reserved fruits and serve with long spoons to mix in the cream.

Fruit-tea smoothie

Depending on your preference you can use any of the varied assortment of fruit teas, now readily available in most large supermarkets, for this thick, creamy blend. This recipe uses dried apricots and apples but you could easily replace these with dried pears, peaches or tropical dried fruits. From start to finish, this smoothie takes about one hour to prepare, so make sure you don't leave this one until the last minute.

Makes 2 glasses

50g/2oz dried apples
25g/1oz dried apricots
2 fruit teabags
juice of 1 lemon
30ml/2 tbsp crème fraîche or natural
    (plain) yogurt
mineral water (optional)

Cook's tip
Apple and lemon, apple and mango, forest berries and strawberry and raspberry fruit teas are just a few that are readily available. When choosing the dried fruit, pick the types that will work best with the flavours in your tea.

1 Using a small, sharp knife, roughly chop the dried apples and apricots. Steep the teabags in 300ml/½ pint/ 1¼ cups boiling water for 5 minutes, then remove the teabags.

2 Add the chopped fruit to the tea and leave to stand for 30 minutes. Chill in the refrigerator for about 30 minutes until the tea is completely cold.

3 Put the fruit and tea mixture into a blender or food processor and add the lemon juice. Blend well until smooth, scraping the mixture down from the side of the bowl, if necessary.

4 Add the crème fraîche or yogurt and blend briefly, adding a little mineral water if the smoothie is too thick. Serve in tall glasses.

Smooth and simple Energy 159kcal/669kJ; Protein 2.5g; Carbohydrate 29.7g, of which sugars 29.7g; Fat 4.1g, of which saturates 2.4g; Cholesterol 11mg; Calcium 60mg; Fibre 1.9g; Sodium 26mg.
Fruit-tea smoothie Energy 116kcal/486kJ; Protein 1.9g; Carbohydrate 14.1g, of which sugars 14g; Fat 6.2g, of which saturates 4.1g; Cholesterol 17mg; Calcium 36mg; Fibre 2.4g; Sodium 9mg.

Purple haze

Thick, dark blueberry purée swirled into pale and creamy vanilla-flavoured buttermilk looks stunning and tastes simply divine. Despite its creaminess, the buttermilk gives this sumptuous smoothie a delicious sharp tang. If you do not like buttermilk or cannot find it in your local supermarket, you could use a mixture of half yogurt and half milk instead.

Makes 2 tall glasses

250g/9oz/2¼ cups blueberries
50g/2oz/¼ cup caster (superfine) sugar
15ml/1 tbsp lemon juice
300ml/½ pint/1¼ cups buttermilk
5ml/1 tsp vanilla extract
150ml/¼ pint/⅔ cup full cream (whole) milk

1 Push the blueberries through a juicer and stir in 15ml/1 tbsp of the sugar and the lemon juice. Stir well and divide between two tall glasses.

2 Put the buttermilk, vanilla extract, milk and remaining sugar in a blender or food processor and blend until really frothy. (Alternatively, use a hand-held electric blender and blend until the mixture froths up.)

3 Pour the buttermilk mixture over the blueberry juice so the mixtures swirl together naturally – there is no need to stir them together as it tastes and looks better if they remain separate to a certain degree. Serve immediately.

Cook's tip
Deep violet blueberry juice makes a fantastic contrast in both colour and flavour to the buttermilk. If you cannot get hold of blueberries, other slightly tart fruits such as raspberries or blackberries would also work in this creamy combination.

Purple haze Energy 274kcal/1157kJ; Protein 9.1g; Carbohydrate 54.2g, of which sugars 49.2g; Fat 3.9g, of which saturates 2.4g; Cholesterol 13mg; Calcium 284mg; Fibre 2.5g; Sodium 99mg.

Very berry

Fresh and frozen cranberries are often in short supply, but dried berries are available all year round and make a tasty dairy-free shake when combined with soya milk. Tiny crimson redcurrants make the perfect partner for the dried cranberries in this refreshingly tart, sparkling smoothie, and this low-fat blend is packed with natural sugars, essential nutrients and vitamins.

Makes 1 large glass

25g/1oz/¼ cup dried cranberries
150g/5oz/1¼ cups redcurrants, plus extra
  to decorate
10ml/2 tsp clear honey
50ml/2fl oz/¼ cup soya milk
sparkling mineral water

1 Put the cranberries in a small bowl, pour over 90ml/6 tbsp boiling water and leave to stand for 10 minutes.

2 String the redcurrants by drawing the stems through the tines of a fork to pull off the delicate currants.

3 Put the currants in a food processor or blender with the cranberries and soaking water. Blend well until smooth.

4 Add the honey and soya milk and whizz briefly to combine the ingredients.

5 Pour the berry shake into a large glass, then top with a little sparkling mineral water to lighten the drink. Drape the redcurrants decoratively over the edge of the glass and serve the smoothie immediately.

Cook's tip
Allowing time for the dried cranberries to rehydrate means they will become plump and juicy – making them much easier to blend and maximizing their flavour.

Very berry Energy 126kcal/539kJ; Protein 3.8g; Carbohydrate 27.1g, of which sugars 27.1g; Fat 1g, of which saturates 0.1g; Cholesterol 0mg; Calcium 115mg; Fibre 7g; Sodium 25mg.

Raspberry, apple and rose water smoothie

Although usually put through the juicer for drinking, apples can be blended as long as you process them well to ensure a really flavour-packed smoothie. This recipe is thinned with fresh apple juice, which can be either shop-bought (make sure it is good quality) or home-made.

Makes 2 glasses

2 eating apples
10ml/2 tsp caster (superfine) sugar
15ml/1 tbsp lemon juice
130g/4½oz/¾ cup fresh or frozen raspberries
150ml/¼ pint/⅔ cup apple juice
15–30ml/1–2 tbsp rose water
whole raspberries and rose petals,
    to decorate (optional)

Cook's tip
If you prefer raspberries without the pips (seeds), blend them first and then push the purée through a sieve (strainer) to remove the pips before mixing it with the apples.

1 Peel and core the apples and put in a blender or food processor with the sugar and lemon juice. Blend well until smooth, scraping the mixture down from the side of the bowl, if necessary.

2 Add the raspberries and apple juice to the apple purée and blend until completely smooth.

3 Add the rose water to the smoothie and blend briefly to combine.

4 Pour the smoothie into two medium glasses and place whole raspberries and rose petals on top of the drinks to decorate, if you like. Serve the smoothie immediately, or chill in the refrigerator until ready to serve.

Coconut and hazelnut smoothie

This intensely nutty, rich and creamy drink is one to sip at your leisure. Leftovers can be put in the refrigerator for up to a couple of days, in which time the flavour of the hazelnuts will develop.

Makes 2 glasses

90g/3½oz/scant 1 cup whole
    blanched hazelnuts
25g/1oz/2 tbsp golden caster
    (superfine) sugar
2.5ml/½ tsp almond extract
200ml/7fl oz/scant 1 cup coconut cream
30ml/2 tbsp double (heavy) cream (optional)
150ml/¼ pint/⅔ cup mineral water
crushed ice

Cook's tip
If you want a frothy topping on this creamy smoothie, whisk it using a handheld electric wand after adding the mineral water, before pouring into the glasses.

1 Roughly chop the hazelnuts and lightly toast them in a small frying pan, turning frequently. Leave to cool, then put the nuts into a blender or food processor with the caster sugar and blend well until very finely ground.

2 Add the almond extract, coconut cream and double cream, if using, and blend thoroughly until smooth.

3 Strain the mixture through a sieve (strainer) into a jug (pitcher), pressing the pulp down with the back of a spoon to extract as much juice as possible. Stir in the mineral water.

4 Half-fill two glasses with crushed ice and pour over the nut smoothie. Serve the drinks immediately, or chill in the refrigerator until ready to serve.

Raspberry smoothie Energy 91kcal/391kJ; Protein 1.3g; Carbohydrate 22.3g, of which sugars 22.3g; Fat 0.4g, of which saturates 0.1g; Cholesterol 0mg; Calcium 27mg; Fibre 2.9g; Sodium 6mg.
Coconut smoothie Energy 364kcal/1514kJ; Protein 6.7g; Carbohydrate 20.7g, of which sugars 19.8g; Fat 28.9g, of which saturates 2.3g; Cholesterol 0mg; Calcium 99mg; Fibre 2.9g; Sodium 114mg.

Red defender

Boost your body's defences with this delicious blend of red fruits. Fresh watermelon, strawberries and grapes are an excellent source of vitamin C and the black watermelon seeds, like many other seeds, are rich in essential nutrients. If you really don't like the idea of blending the seeds, remove them first.

1 Hull the strawberries and halve them if they are large. Pull the grapes from their stalks. Cut away the skin from the watermelon.

2 Put the watermelon in a blender or food processor and blend until the seeds are broken up. Add the strawberries and grapes and blend until completely smooth, scraping the mixture down from the side of the bowl, if necessary. Serve in chunky glasses.

Makes 2 glasses

200g/7oz/1¾ cups strawberries
small bunch red grapes, about 90g/3½oz
1 small wedge of watermelon

Cook's tip
Decorate this juice with chunks of watermelon or strawberry halves.

Red defender Energy 85kcal/362kJ; Protein 1.5g; Carbohydrate 20.1g, of which sugars 20.1g; Fat 0.5g, of which saturates 0.1g; Cholesterol 0mg; Calcium 29mg; Fibre 1.5g; Sodium 9mg.

Green devil

Choose a well-flavoured avocado, such as a knobbly, dark-skinned Hass, for this slightly spicy, hot and sour smoothie. Cucumber adds a refreshing edge, while lemon and lime juice zip up the flavour, and the chilli sauce adds an irresistible fiery bite. This is one little devil that is sure to liven up even the most lethargic days.

Makes 2–3 glasses

1 small ripe avocado
½ cucumber
30ml/2 tbsp lemon juice
30ml/2 tbsp lime juice
10ml/2 tsp caster (superfine) sugar
pinch of salt
250ml/8fl oz/1 cup apple juice or
 mineral water
10–20ml/2–4 tsp sweet chilli sauce
ice cubes
red chilli curls, to decorate

2 Process the ingredients until smooth and creamy, then add the apple juice or mineral water and a little of the chilli sauce. Blend once more to lightly mix the ingredients together.

3 Pour the smoothie over ice cubes. Decorate with red chilli curls and serve with stirrers and extra chilli sauce.

1 Halve the avocado and use a sharp knife to remove the stone (pit). Scoop the flesh from both halves into a blender or food processor. Peel and roughly chop the cucumber and add to the blender or food processor, then add the lemon and lime juice, the caster sugar and a little salt.

Cook's tip

To make chilli curls, core and seed a fresh red chilli and cut it into very fine strips. Put the strips in a bowl of iced water and leave to stand for 20 minutes or until the strips curl. Use them to decorate this smoothie.

 Seductively smooth avocados are as good for you as they taste. Their fresh vitamin- and mineral-rich flesh is reputed to be fantastic for healthy hair and skin.

Green devil Energy 143kcal/598kJ; Protein 1.3g; Carbohydrate 13.2g, of which sugars 12.5g; Fat 9.8g, of which saturates 2.1g; Cholesterol 0mg; Calcium 19mg; Fibre 1.9g; Sodium 6mg.

Thyme-scented plum lush

Make this divine drink in the early autumn when plums are at their sweetest and best.
Their silky smooth flesh blends down to produce the most wonderfully textured smoothie,
while scented lemon thyme and honey complement the flavour perfectly. This luxurious juice
is easy to make and has an irresistible fragrance that is at once warming and refreshing.

Makes 2–3 glasses

400g/14oz red plums
30–45ml/2–3 tbsp clear honey
15ml/1 tbsp chopped fresh lemon thyme,
  plus extra thyme sprigs to decorate
100g/3¾oz crushed ice

Cook's tip
Dark, purplish-red plums, with their almost violet bloom and sweet, intense flavour, juice well and make some of the most tempting and vibrant fruit drinks.

1 Using a sharp knife, halve and stone (pit) the plums and put in a blender or food processor. Add 30ml/2 tbsp of the honey and the lemon thyme and blend until smooth, scraping down the side of the bowl, if necessary.

2 Add the ice and blend until slushy. Taste for sweetness, adding a little more honey if necessary. Pour into glasses and serve immediately, decorated with a sprig of thyme.

Thyme-scented plum lush Energy 77kcal/330kJ; Protein 0.8g; Carbohydrate 19.4g, of which sugars 19.4g; Fat 0.1g, of which saturates 0g; Cholesterol 0mg; Calcium 18mg; Fibre 2.1g; Sodium 4mg.

Fire and ice

Tickle your tastebuds with this unconventional frozen yogurt drink that is flavoured with fresh orange juice and specks of hot red chilli. It's great on a hot summer's day, after lunch or any other time when you're in need of a refreshing boost. If you're in a party mood, add an alcoholic kick to the drink by drizzling each glass with a splash of orange liqueur before serving.

Makes 2–3 tall glasses

90g/3½oz/½ cup caster (superfine) sugar
1 lemon
300ml/½ pint/1¼ cups freshly squeezed
   orange juice
200g/7oz/scant 1 cup Greek (US strained
   plain) yogurt
1 red chilli, seeded and finely chopped
60ml/4 tbsp Cointreau or other orange-
   flavoured liqueur (optional)
orange slices and extra chillies, to decorate

1 Put the sugar in a pan with 100ml/ 3½fl oz/scant ½ cup water and heat gently, stirring with a spoon until the sugar has dissolved. Pour into a freezer container and leave to cool. Finely grate the rind of the lemon and juice.

Cook's tip
Don't worry if you forget to remove the chilli yogurt from the freezer before it has frozen solid. Leave it at room temperature for a while to soften or simply heat it briefly in a microwave.

2 Add the lemon rind and juice and 100ml/3½fl oz/scant ½ cup of the orange juice. Freeze for 2 hours or until a band of ice has formed around the edges. Turn into a bowl and add the yogurt and chopped chilli. Whisk until thick. Freeze for 1–2 hours until almost solid.

3 To serve, scoop the frozen yogurt into a blender or food processor and add the remaining orange juice. Process until very thick and smooth. Pour into tall glasses and drizzle with a little liqueur, if using. Serve with straws and decorate with orange slices and fresh chillies.

Fire and ice Energy 234kcal/989kJ; Protein 5.4g; Carbohydrate 41.6g, of which sugars 41.6g; Fat 7g, of which saturates 3.5g; Cholesterol 0mg; Calcium 131mg; Fibre 0.1g; Sodium 60mg.

cool
creamy
shakes

Milkshakes can be either refreshing and fruity or smooth and creamy, but they are always a treat. Inspiring ingredients include brownies and garden mint, and there are several shakes made with more traditional flavours such as vanilla or banana. Fun for kids and nostalgically appealing for adults, comfort drinks never looked or tasted so good.

Rose petal and almond milk

If you're lucky enough to have a mass of roses in the garden, it's well worth sacrificing a few to make this delicately scented summer smoothie. Thickened and flavoured with ground ratafia biscuits, this fragrant drink is the perfect way to relax on a hot lazy afternoon.

Makes 2 glasses

15g/½oz scented rose petals (preferably pink), plus extra to decorate
300ml/½ pint/1¼ cups milk
25g/1oz ratafia biscuits (almond macaroons)
ice cubes

Cook's tip
If you have bought roses, or even if you have picked them from your own garden, make sure you wash the petals thoroughly before you use them for cooking. This will help to remove any chemicals or pesticides that may have been sprayed on to the flowers.

1 Put the rose petals in a small pan with half the milk and bring just to the boil. Put the ratafia biscuits in a bowl, pour over the hot milk and leave to stand for 10 minutes.

2 Transfer the mixture to a blender or food processor with the remaining milk, and blend until smooth.

3 Strain the milk through a sieve (strainer) into a wide jug (pitcher) to remove any lumps of biscuit or rose petals that have not been blended properly, and chill for at least 1 hour.

4 When the milk is well chilled, pour over ice cubes and serve immediately, decorating with rose petals, if you like.

Banana and maple crunch

Brilliant for making quick and easy blended drinks, bananas have a natural affinity with maple syrup and pecan nuts – what a combination. Serve this creamy, syrupy smoothie over ice and, if you are feeling decadent, dunk in some chunky chocolate cookies to scoop up a mouthful. It is best to serve this smoothie as soon as it is ready because it will not keep well. Finishing it off in one sitting should not be too difficult.

Makes 2 glasses

2 large bananas
50g/2oz/½ cup pecan nuts, plus extra to serve
150ml/¼ pint/⅔ cup full cream (whole) milk
60ml/4 tbsp pure maple syrup
crushed ice

Cook's tips
It is important to use ripe bananas in this recipe and, although you could replace the nuts with another variety such as hazelnuts, the combination of pecans, bananas and maple syrup is such a classic that any variation won't be as good.

1 Put the bananas in a blender or food processor and process until smooth. Add the nuts and blend again until thoroughly combined.

2 The nuts must be finely ground so stop and scrape down the side of the bowl once or twice, if necessary.

3 Add the maple syrup, then pour the milk over the banana paste and blend again until creamy.

4 Half-fill two large glasses with crushed ice and pour the smoothie over the top. Serve sprinkled with extra pecan nuts, if you like.

Rose petal and almond milk Energy 124kcal/523kJ; Protein 5.8g; Carbohydrate 17g, of which sugars 11.5g; Fat 4.2g, of which saturates 2.4g; Cholesterol 9mg; Calcium 197mg; Fibre 0.2g; Sodium 106mg.
Banana and maple crunch Energy 391kcal/1641kJ; Protein 6.2g; Carbohydrate 51.9g, of which sugars 49.2g; Fat 19.1g, of which saturates 2.4g; Cholesterol 4mg; Calcium 116mg; Fibre 2.3g; Sodium 115mg.

Honey and banana milkshake

This delicious drink demonstrates just how smooth and creamy a milkshake can be, even without using dairy produce. Make it using either soya or rice milk together with a vanilla-flavoured, iced non-dairy dessert to achieve a surprisingly rich and creamy flavour. Bananas make a nutritious, energy-boosting addition to drinks – this one is almost a meal in itself.

Makes 2 glasses

2 bananas
30ml/2 tbsp clear honey
15ml/1 tbsp lemon juice
300ml/½ pint/1¼ cups soya or rice milk
4 scoops vanilla iced non-dairy dessert

Cook's tip
If you are happy to use dairy produce, simply use ordinary milk and vanilla ice cream in place of the non-dairy ingredients.

1 Break the bananas into pieces and put in a blender or food processor with the honey and lemon juice. Blend until very smooth, scraping the mixture down from the side of the bowl with a rubber spatula, if necessary.

2 Add the soya or rice milk and two scoops of iced non-dairy dessert, then blend until smooth. Pour into tall glasses and add another scoop of dessert to each. Serve immediately.

Honey and banana milkshake Energy 416kcal/1749kJ; Protein 6.1g; Carbohydrate 68.4g, of which sugars 65.6g; Fat 15g, of which saturates 8.9g; Cholesterol 10mg; Calcium 117mg; Fibre 2.3g; Sodium 81mg.

Stem ginger and pear shake

Although fresh fruit cannot be beaten for its flavour and nutritional value, canned varieties are a good store-cupboard stand-by for when you've run out of fresh. They are still nutritionally sound, particularly if packed in natural, unsweetened fruit juice. Preserved stem ginger makes the perfect partner to pears in this taste-tingling, creamy creation.

1 Shave off some wafer-thin slices from one of the pieces of ginger and reserve. Roughly chop the remaining ginger. Drain the pears, reserving about 150ml/¼ pint/⅔ cup of the juice.

2 Put the pears, measured juice and chopped ginger in a blender or food processor and blend until smooth, scraping the mixture down from the side of the bowl, if necessary.

3 Strain through a sieve (strainer) into a jug (pitcher). Whisk in the milk, cream and ginger syrup and pour into two glasses. Serve scattered with the ginger shavings.

Makes 2 glasses

3 pieces (about 65g/2½oz) preserved stem
    ginger, plus 30ml/2 tbsp ginger syrup from
    the jar
400g/14oz can pears in natural fruit juice
150ml/¼ pint/⅔ cup full cream (whole) milk
100ml/3½fl oz/scant ½ cup single
    (light) cream
ice cubes

Cook's tip
If you like your milkshake really smooth, strain the pear mixture through a sieve (strainer) to remove any bits of fibre that might remain in the pears. However, if you like the consistency of the stringy bits, skip this part of the recipe.

Stem ginger and pear shake Energy 257kcal/1077kJ; Protein 4.8g; Carbohydrate 33.4g, of which sugars 33.4g; Fat 12.5g, of which saturates 8g; Cholesterol 38mg; Calcium 148mg; Fibre 2.8g; Sodium 94mg.

Lemon meringue

Just as lemon meringue pie is a favourite dessert, this wonderful milkshake is sure to become a favourite drink. The blend of sweet meringue and lemon is carefully balanced in a velvety smooth, ice-cool drink that is not too rich and surprisingly refreshing. This really is a dessert in a glass and will undoubtedly go down well at your next dinner party.

2 Coarsely crush 15g/½oz of the meringues and reserve for decoration. Break the remainder into a blender or food processor. Add the lemon syrup and blend until smooth.

3 With the machine still running, gradually pour in the milk until the mixture is pale and frothy. Add the ice cream and blend again until smooth.

4 Pour the milkshake into glasses and decorate the sides with lemon slices or twists of lemon peel. Scatter the reserved meringue on top and serve immediately with spoons.

Makes 2 glasses

30ml/2 tbsp caster (superfine) sugar
3 lemons
50g/2oz crisp white meringues
300ml/½ pint/1¼ cups full cream (whole) milk
2 scoops vanilla ice cream
lemon slices or twists of peel,
   to decorate

1 Put the sugar in a small pan with 100ml/3½fl oz/scant ½ cup water and heat gently until the sugar dissolves. Pour into a jug (pitcher). Squeeze the lemons using a citrus juicer and add the juice to the syrup. Leave to cool.

Cook's tip
When shopping for the lemons to decorate this drink, be sure to buy the unwaxed variety.

Lemon meringue Energy 331kcal/1398kJ; Protein 8.5g; Carbohydrate 55.2g, of which sugars 55.1g; Fat 10.1g, of which saturates 6.2g; Cholesterol 9mg; Calcium 241mg; Fibre 0g; Sodium 125mg.

Garden mint milkshake

If you have mint growing in your garden, pick some for this recipe, as the fresher the mint, the better the flavour will be. The mint is infused in a sugar syrup, then left to cool before being blended to an aromatic, frothy shake with yogurt and creamy milk. The final milkshake is speckled with tiny green flecks, but if you prefer a completely smooth texture, you can strain these out.

Makes 2 glasses

25g/1oz/1 cup fresh mint
50g/2oz/¼ cup caster (superfine) sugar
200g/7oz/scant 1 cup natural
   (plain) yogurt
200ml/7fl oz/scant 1 cup full cream
   (whole) milk
15ml/1 tbsp lemon juice
crushed ice cubes
icing (confectioners') sugar, to decorate

2 Heat the mixture, stirring occasionally, until the sugar dissolves, then boil for 2 minutes. Remove the pan from the heat and set aside until the syrup is completely cool.

3 Strain the cooled syrup through a sieve (strainer) into a jug (pitcher), pressing the mint against the side of the sieve with the back of a spoon. Pour into a blender or food processor.

4 Add the yogurt and milk to the syrup and blend until smooth and frothy. Add two of the reserved mint sprigs and the lemon juice and blend until the milkshake is specked with tiny green flecks.

5 Put the crushed ice in tall glasses or tumblers and pour over the milkshake. Dust the mint sprigs with icing sugar and use to decorate the glasses. Serve.

1 Pull out four small mint sprigs and set aside. Roughly snip the remaining leaves into a small pan. Add the sugar and pour over 105ml/7 tbsp water.

Garden mint milkshake Energy 299kcal/1272kJ; Protein 8.8g; Carbohydrate 64.5g, of which sugars 64.5g; Fat 2.7g, of which saturates 1.6g; Cholesterol 7mg; Calcium 337mg; Fibre 0g; Sodium 129mg.

Rosemary and almond cream

This delightful concoction is definitely one to choose if you are looking for something a little different. Fresh sprigs of rosemary, infused in milk, provide a gentle fragrance and flavour that blends deliciously with the sweet ratafia biscuits. Frothed up with creamy, melting vanilla ice cream, this velvety smooth creation is quite simply superb.

Makes 2 glasses

4 long sprigs of fresh rosemary
400ml/14fl oz/1⅔ cups full cream (whole) milk
50g/2oz ratafia biscuits (almond macaroons) or amaretti, plus extra to decorate
3 large scoops vanilla ice cream
frosted rosemary sprigs, to decorate

Cook's tip
To make frosted rosemary sprigs, lightly coat the sprigs in a little beaten egg white. Dip in caster (superfine) sugar and leave to dry.

1 Put the rosemary sprigs in a small pan. Add 150ml/¼ pint/⅔ cup of the milk and heat very gently until the milk begins to boil. Remove the pan from the heat and pour the mixture into a bowl. Leave to cool for 10 minutes.

2 Remove the rosemary sprigs and carefully pour the still warm milk into a blender or food processor. Add the ratafia biscuits and blend until smooth and creamy. Add the remaining 250ml/8fl oz/1 cup milk and blend the mixture thoroughly.

3 Scoop the vanilla ice cream into the milk and biscuit mixture and blend until it is fully incorporated. Pour into large glasses and serve the milkshake immediately, decorating the top of each glass with delicate frosted rosemary sprigs and a few pieces of crumbled ratafia biscuits.

Pistachio thick-shake

Don't be put off by the presence of rice in this lovely, layered dairy-free milkshake. Blended with soya milk, pistachio nuts and non-dairy ice cream, it makes a dreamy, creamy blend that can be sipped, layer by layer, or swirled together with a pretty stirrer. As its name suggests, this shake is wonderfully rich and decadent; serve it in tall narrow glasses.

Makes 3–4 small glasses

550ml/18fl oz/2½ cups soya milk
50g/2oz/generous ¼ cup pudding rice
60ml/4 tbsp caster (superfine) sugar
finely grated rind of 1 lemon
75g/3oz/¾ cup shelled pistachio nuts, plus extra to decorate
300ml/10fl oz vanilla iced non-dairy dessert
5ml/1 tsp almond extract

1 Put the soya milk in a large, heavy pan with the rice, sugar and lemon rind. Bring slowly to the boil, then reduce the heat to simmer. Partially cover the pan with a lid and cook on the lowest heat for about 30 minutes, or until the rice is completely tender.

2 Transfer the rice to a heatproof bowl and leave to stand until completely cold.

3 Put the pistachio nuts in another heatproof bowl and cover with boiling water. Leave to stand for about 2 minutes and then drain.

4 Rub the pistachio nuts between several layers of kitchen paper to loosen the skins, then peel them away. (Don't worry about removing every bit of skin, but getting most of it off will make a prettier coloured milkshake.)

5 Put the cold rice into a blender or food processor and blend until smooth. Put half the mixture in a bowl. Add the non-dairy dessert to the blender and blend until smooth. Pour into a separate bowl. Add the nuts, the reserved rice and the almond extract to the blender and process until the nuts are finely

6 Layer the two mixtures in glasses and serve decorated with extra pistachios.

Rosemary and almond cream Energy 400kcal/1684kJ; Protein 12.3g; Carbohydrate 51.5g, of which sugars 39.4g; Fat 16.4g, of which saturates 10.5g; Cholesterol 39mg; Calcium 385mg; Fibre 0.4g; Sodium 236mg.
Pistachio thick-shake Energy 397kcal/1660kJ; Protein 11.4g; Carbohydrate 47.1g, of which sugars 34.1g; Fat 18.6g, of which saturates 4.8g; Cholesterol 5mg; Calcium 154mg; Fibre 1.2g; Sodium 189mg.

Marzipan and orange crush

The wintry scents and flavours of juicy oranges and marzipan make an interesting combination and the citrus juice adds a delicious refreshing tang to an otherwise very rich, creamy drink. It's a great blend to make if you are entertaining friends as its unusual blend of ingredients is sure to be a talking point. Make plenty of this irresistible shake and chill whatever you don't use in the refrigerator for another time.

Makes 3–4 glasses

130g/4½oz marzipan
finely grated rind and juice of 2 large oranges
juice of 1 lemon
150ml/¼ pint/⅔ cup mineral water
150ml/¼ pint/⅔ cup single (light) cream
ice cubes
orange wedges, to decorate (optional)

Cook's tip
Give this drink a whisk before serving, as it may have settled.

1 Break the marzipan into small pieces and put in a blender or food processor. Add the orange rind and juice along with the lemon juice. Blend the mixture thoroughly until smooth.

2 Add the mineral water and cream and blend again until smooth and frothy. Pour over ice cubes in glasses and serve decorated with the orange wedges, if you like.

Cherry and coconut shake

The season for fresh cherries is all too short, but canned cherries make a very good and surprisingly delicious stand-by. Here they are combined in a classic partnership with creamy coconut milk to make a rich, fruity drink that is perfect for people who are not too keen on really sweet, thick milkshakes. Make sure you buy pitted cherries, otherwise you will have to carefully stone them yourself before putting them into the blender.

Makes 2 glasses

425g/15oz can pitted black cherries
    in syrup
200ml/7fl oz/scant 1 cup coconut milk
15ml/1 tbsp light muscovado (brown) sugar
150ml/¼ pint/⅔ cup black cherry-flavour
    yogurt
100ml/3½fl oz/scant ½ cup double
    (heavy) cream
lightly toasted shredded coconut,
    to decorate

Cook's tip
If you can't get black cherry-flavour yogurt, use a vanilla or natural (plain) yogurt instead and add a little extra sugar when blending.

1 Put the canned cherries into a sieve (strainer) over a bowl to drain. Reserve the syrup for later.

2 Put the drained cherries in a blender or food processor with the coconut milk and sugar and blend briefly until fairly smooth. (Do not be tempted to over-blend the mixture or it may begin to separate.)

3 Pour the mixture through a sieve into a jug (pitcher), pressing the pulp down into the sieve with the back of a spoon to extract as much juice as possible.

4 Add the reserved cherry syrup, yogurt and cream and whisk lightly until smooth and frothy. Pour into glasses and scatter with shredded coconut.

Marzipan and orange crush Energy 208kcal/871kJ; Protein 3.1g; Carbohydrate 25g, of which sugars 25g; Fat 11.3g, of which saturates 4.9g; Cholesterol 21mg; Calcium 57mg; Fibre 0.7g; Sodium 20mg.
Cherry and coconut shake Energy 518kcal/2176kJ; Protein 5.3g; Carbohydrate 66.4g, of which sugars 66.4g; Fat 27.7g, of which saturates 17.2g; Cholesterol 72mg; Calcium 202mg; Fibre 1.3g; Sodium 187mg.

Passionata

The combination of ripe passion fruit and fresh oranges with sweet caramel is gorgeous in this dreamy milkshake. For convenience, you can easily make the caramel syrup and combine it with the fresh passion fruit juice in advance, so it's all ready for blending with the milk. For the best results make sure you use really ripe, crinkly passion fruit.

Makes 4 glasses

90g/3½oz/½ cup caster (superfine) sugar
juice of 2 large oranges
juice of 1 lemon
6 ripe passion fruit, plus extra for garnish
550ml/18fl oz/2½ cups full cream
   (whole) milk
ice cubes

1 Put the sugar in a small, heavy pan with 200ml/7fl oz/scant 1 cup water. Heat gently, stirring with a wooden spoon until the sugar has dissolved.

2 Bring the mixture to the boil and cook, without stirring, for about 5 minutes until the syrup has turned to a deep golden caramel. Watch closely towards the end of the cooking time as caramel can burn very quickly. If this happens, let the caramel cool, then throw it away and start again.

3 When the caramel has turned a deep golden colour, immediately lower the base of the pan into cold water to prevent it from cooking any further.

4 Carefully add the orange and lemon juice, standing back slightly as the mixture will splutter. Return the pan to the heat and cook gently, stirring continuously, to make a smooth syrup. Transfer the syrup to a small heatproof bowl and set aside until it has cooled completely.

5 Halve the passion fruit and scoop the seeds into a blender or food processor. Add the caramel and milk and blend until smooth and frothy. Pour over ice and serve with a passion fruit garnish.

Passionata Energy 197kcal/828kJ; Protein 5.4g; Carbohydrate 33.2g, of which sugars 33.2g; Fat 5.5g, of which saturates 3.5g; Cholesterol 19mg; Calcium 179mg; Fibre 0.8g; Sodium 67mg.

Rocky river

This rich, sweet milkshake combines chilled custard with decadent chocolate, chunky nuts and delicious marshmallows. It is great fun to make with children, who will enjoy its sticky, indulgent sweetness almost as much as the adults. Prepare this shake whenever you're really in need of a treat or when relaxing in the garden on a hot afternoon.

Makes 3 glasses

75g/3oz plain (semisweet) chocolate
40g/1½oz/scant ½ cup blanched almonds
50g/2oz pink and white marshmallows
600ml/1 pint/2½ cups good quality
   ready-made custard
300ml/½ pint/1¼ cups milk
30ml/2 tbsp caster (superfine) sugar
5ml/1 tsp vanilla extract

4 Pour into big glasses and serve immediately, sprinkled with the reserved marshmallows and grated chocolate.

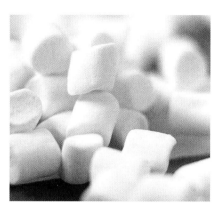

Cook's tip
Very cold chocolate can be difficult to grate. You might find it easier if you microwave it, very briefly, as this will make the chocolate less brittle for grating.

1 Coarsely grate the chocolate. Lightly toast the almonds, then chop them. Cut the marshmallows roughly into pieces, using scissors, reserving a few pieces for decoration.

2 Put the custard into a blender or food processor and add the milk, sugar and vanilla extract. Blend briefly to combine.

3 Reserve a little chocolate for sprinkling, then add the remainder to the blender with the almonds and marshmallows. Blend until the marshmallows are chopped into small pieces.

Rocky river Energy 545kcal/2296kJ; Protein 13.6g; Carbohydrate 78.4g, of which sugars 67.7g; Fat 19.7g, of which saturates 5.9g; Cholesterol 12mg; Calcium 348mg; Fibre 1.8g; Sodium 134mg.

Cinnamon iced coffee

When the weather warms up, swap mugs of hot coffee for this treat of a summer cooler. Lightly flavoured with cinnamon and served icy cold, it's a smooth relaxing drink for when you need to unwind – and it's well worth keeping a jug in the refrigerator.

Makes 2 large glasses

5ml/1 tsp ground cinnamon
400ml/14fl oz/1⅔ cups full cream (whole) milk
40g/1½oz/3 tbsp caster (superfine) sugar
300ml/½ pint/1¼ cups strong cold espresso coffee
ice cubes
cinnamon sticks, to serve

Cook's tip
For a dinner party, why not spice things up and serve these shakes with a large dash of Bailey's or Tia Maria. These types of alcohol work particularly well with this drink's creaminess and its subtle cinnamon tones.

1 Put the cinnamon and 100ml/3½fl oz/ scant ½ cup of the milk in a small pan with the sugar. Bring the milk slowly to the boil then remove from the heat and leave to cool.

2 Turn the cinnamon milk into a large jug (pitcher) or bowl. Add the remaining milk and the coffee and whisk well, using a hand-held electric wand, until frothy. Pour into glasses with ice and serve with cinnamon sticks for stirrers.

Cinnamon iced coffee Energy 218kcal/915kJ; Protein 7.1g; Carbohydrate 30.8g, of which sugars 29.9g; Fat 8.2g, of which saturates 5.1g; Cholesterol 28mg; Calcium 251mg; Fibre 0g; Sodium 88mg.

Chocolate brownie milkshake

For a truly indulgent flavour, use home-made chocolate brownies in this fabulously tasty milkshake. It is very rich – and incredibly decadent – so sit back, relax and just enjoy a totally luxurious moment on your own – well, you wouldn't want to share it.

1 Crumble the chocolate brownies into a blender or food processor and add the milk. Blend until the mixture is a pale chocolate colour.

2 Add the ice cream and blend until smooth and frothy. Pour into a tall glass and spoon over a little whipped cream. Serve scattered with chocolate shavings or a dusting of cocoa powder.

Makes 1 large glass

40g/1½oz chocolate brownies
200ml/7fl oz/scant 1 cup full cream
  (whole) milk
2 scoops vanilla ice cream
a little whipped cream
chocolate shavings or cocoa powder
  (unsweetened), to decorate

Cook's tip
If you fancy treating yourself to a milkshake that's even more chocolatey than this one, replace the vanilla ice cream with the same amount of a chocolate or chocolate-chip variety.

Chocolate brownie milkshake Energy 637kcal/2652kJ; Protein 15.4g; Carbohydrate 54.4g, of which sugars 45.5g; Fat 41g, of which saturates 18.6g; Cholesterol 28mg; Calcium 416mg; Fibre 0g; Sodium 348mg.

drinks
for
kids

Drinks for breakfast, after school or even kids'
parties are transformed with these delicious
concoctions. There are fresh fruit smoothies, fun
floats and shakes, and some real tea-time treats
that could quite easily take the place of an ordinary
dessert or pudding. Let the kids help prepare them
and they'll enjoy these blends even more.

Raspberry, banana and peach smoothie

Children will love this naturally sweet fruit drink. Whizzed up in just a matter of minutes, this thick, slightly tart smoothie makes a good stop-gap between meals, a brilliant, easy-to-eat breakfast or serves as a healthy – and very tasty – dessert.

1 Halve, stone (pit) and roughly chop the peach, break the banana into pieces and put both fruits in a blender or food processor. Blend until smooth, scraping the mixture down the side of the bowl, if necessary.

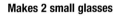

2 Add the raspberries and blend until smooth. Pour into glasses and top up with mineral water, if using. Add ice cubes, decorate with extra raspberries and serve with straws or spoons.

Makes 2 small glasses

1 large ripe peach
1 small banana
130g/4½oz/¾ cup fresh or frozen
    raspberries, plus extra to decorate
still or sparkling mineral water (optional)
ice cubes

Cook's tip
If your children dislike the pips (seeds) in raspberries, blend them first and push the mixture through a fine sieve (strainer) to remove the seeds, then return the purée to the blended banana mixture.

Raspberry, banana and peach smoothie Energy 66kcal/282kJ; Protein 1.8g; Carbohydrate 15g, of which sugars 14g; Fat 0.4g, of which saturates 0.1g; Cholesterol 0mg; Calcium 21mg; Fibre 2.6g; Sodium 3mg.

Top pops

Chunky ice-lolly stirrers give this fruit-packed smoothie plenty of child-appeal. It's great for a party or as an after-school treat on a hot day. The lollies can be frozen ahead and stored so they're ready on demand, and the juice takes just moments to prepare.

Makes 2 glasses

1 apple
300ml/½ pint/1¼ cups apple juice
2 kiwi fruit
90g/3½oz/generous ½ cup raspberries
10ml/2 tsp caster (superfine) sugar
150g/5oz/1 cup red grapes
150g/5oz/1¼ cups blackcurrants or
  blackberries
1 large banana

1 Peel, core and roughly chop the apple. Place in a food processor or blender with 100ml/3½fl oz/ scant ½ cup of the apple juice and blend to a smooth purée. Pour into a third of the sections of an ice-cube tray.

2 Peel and roughly chop the kiwi fruit and blend until smooth with half the remaining apple juice. Pour into another third of the ice-cube tray sections.

3 Blend the raspberries with the sugar and the remaining apple juice and spoon into the final sections. Freeze the tray for about 30 minutes then push a wooden ice-lolly (popsicle) stick into each. Freeze until solid.

4 Put the grapes, blackcurrants or blackberries, and banana into the blender or food processor and blend until smooth. If you like, push the mixture through a coarse sieve (strainer) after blending to remove the seeds and skins.

5 Push several of the fruit lollies out of the tray and place on separate plates for each child. Pour the fruit juice into two glasses and place on plates with the lollies. Serve immediately as the lollies will start to melt very quickly – and don't forget to supply the children with plenty of napkins.

Top pops Energy 231kcal/986kJ; Protein 3g; Carbohydrate 56.2g, of which sugars 55.1g; Fat 1g, of which saturates 0.1g; Cholesterol 0mg; Calcium 84mg; Fibre 6.1g; Sodium 11mg..

Tropical fruit shake

Sweet, fruity and packed with vitamin C, this is a brilliant way to get children to enjoy healthy drinks. If you use really ripe fruit, it shouldn't need any additional sweetening, but taste it to check before serving. Mango makes a thick purée when blended, so top it up with mineral water – or try a good quality lemonade instead.

Makes 2 glasses

½ small pineapple
small bunch seedless white grapes
1 mango
mineral water or lemonade (optional)

2 Process thoroughly until really smooth, scraping the mixture down from the side of the bowl. Pour into glasses, add ice cubes, and top up with mineral water or lemonade, if using. Serve immediately.

Cook's tip
For really fussy children, you might want to strain the mixture first. To do this, push it through a fine sieve (strainer), pressing the pulp in the sieve with the back of a spoon to extract as much juice as possible. Follow the recipe as normal, topping up the glasses with mineral water or lemonade if your children prefer it. To make a novelty decoration, thread pieces of fruit on to straws before you serve the shake.

1 Using a sharp knife, cut away the skin from the pineapple and halve the fruit. Discard the core and roughly chop the flesh of one half. Add to a blender or food processor with the grapes. Halve the mango either side of the flat stone (pit). Scoop the flesh into the blender.

Tropical fruit shake Energy 129kcal/553kJ; Protein 1.3g; Carbohydrate 32.3g, of which sugars 32g; Fat 0.4g, of which saturates 0.1g; Cholesterol 0mg; Calcium 37mg; Fibre 3.7g; Sodium 5mg.

Raspberry rippler

Colourful ripples of raspberry and mango give instant child appeal to this fruit-packed smoothie. Soya milk is so delicious and such a healthy alternative to cow's milk in drinks that it's worth trying, even for children who are not on a dairy-free diet. Here it's blended with mango to create a smooth, thick contrast to the tangy raspberries. For best results, use only really ripe, sweet mango.

Makes 2 glasses

90g/3½oz/generous ½ cup fresh or frozen
   raspberries, plus a few extra to decorate
15–30ml/1–2 tbsp clear honey
1 mango
100ml/3½fl oz/scant ½ cup soya milk

1 Process the raspberries in a blender or food processor until smooth. Add 15ml/1 tbsp water and 5–10ml/1–2 tsp of the honey to sweeten. Transfer to a small bowl and rinse out the blender or food processor bowl.

2 Halve the mango either side of the flat stone (pit). Scoop the flesh from the two halves and around the stone into the clean blender or food processor and process until smooth. Add the soya milk and 10–20ml/2–4 tsp honey to sweeten.

Cook's tip

It will make such a difference to your children's health, and to their general appreciation of food, if they can enjoy fresh, naturally sweet drinks like this. Try serving this smoothie as a refreshing dessert after a barbecue or a family meal – it makes a delicious alternative to the similarly named, but slightly less healthy, raspberry ripple ice cream.

3 Pour a 2.5cm/1in layer of the mango purée into two tumblers. Spoon half the raspberry purée on top. Add the remaining mango purée, then finish with the remaining raspberry purée. Using a teaspoon, lightly swirl the two mixtures together. Serve decorated with extra raspberries.

Raspberry rippler Energy 92kcal/391kJ; Protein 2.7g; Carbohydrate 18.8g, of which sugars 18.6g; Fat 1.1g, of which saturates 0.3g; Cholesterol 0mg; Calcium 27mg; Fibre 3.1g; Sodium 20mg.

Peppermint crush

The next time you see seaside rock or the peppermint candy canes that are around at Christmas time, buy a few sticks for this incredibly easy, fun drink for children. All you need to do is whizz it up with some milk and freeze until slushy, so it's ready and waiting for thirsty youngsters. This shake could also pass as a dessert, so try serving it after a meal.

Makes 4 glasses

90g/3½oz pink peppermint rock (rock candy)
750ml/1¼ pints/3 cups full cream (whole) or
    semi-skimmed (low-fat) milk
a few drops of pink food colouring (optional)
pink candy canes, to serve

Cook's tip

If you cannot find pink candy canes to use as novelty stirrers for this drink, buy peppermint lollipops instead.

1 While the rock is still in its wrapper, hit with a rolling pin to break into small bits. (If unwrapped, put the rock in a polythene bag to crush it.) Transfer the pieces into a blender or food processor.

2 Add the milk and a few drops of pink food colouring, if using, to the crushed rock and process until the rock is broken up into tiny pieces.

3 Pour the mixture into a shallow freezer container and freeze for about 2 hours or until turning slushy around the edges. Beat the mixture with a fork, breaking up the semi-frozen areas and stirring them into the centre.

4 Re-freeze and repeat the process once or twice more until the mixture is slushy. Spoon into glasses and serve with candy cane stirrers.

Peppermint crush Energy 160kcal/679kJ; Protein 6.4g; Carbohydrate 28.4g, of which sugars 28.3g; Fat 3.2g, of which saturates 2g; Cholesterol 11mg; Calcium 226mg; Fibre 0g; Sodium 86mg.

Candystripe

This wickedly indulgent drink combines freshly blended strawberries with a marshmallow flavoured cream, making a milkshake that adults as well as kids will find totally irresistible. There's no point even trying to resist the melting marshmallow sweetness of this cheeky little strawberry confection – just sit back and give yourself up.

Makes 4 large glasses

150g/5oz white and pink marshmallows
500ml/17fl oz/generous 2 cups full cream (whole) milk
60ml/4 tbsp redcurrant jelly
450g/1lb/4 cups strawberries
60ml/4 tbsp double (heavy) cream
extra strawberries and marshmallows, to decorate

1 Put the marshmallows in a heavy pan with half the milk and heat gently, stirring frequently until the marshmallows have melted. Leave to stand until it has cooled.

2 Heat the redcurrant jelly in a small pan until melted. Put the strawberries in a blender or food processor and process until smooth, scraping down the side of the bowl with a rubber spatula as often as is necessary.

3 Stir 10ml/2 tsp of the strawberry purée into the melted jelly. Set aside the strawberry syrup. Pour the remaining purée into a jug (pitcher) and add the marshmallow mixture, the cream and the remaining milk. Chill the milkshake and four large glasses for about 1 hour.

4 To serve, use a teaspoon to drizzle lines of the strawberry syrup down the insides of the glasses – this creates a candystripe effect when filled. Fill the glasses with the milkshake. Serve topped with the extra marshmallows and strawberries and drizzle with any leftover strawberry syrup.

Cook's tip
If you can convince the children to wait long enough, this blend will really benefit from being chilled in the refrigerator for a couple of hours before serving.

Candystripe Energy 349kcal/1467kJ; Protein 6.8g; Carbohydrate 54.2g, of which sugars 47.2g; Fat 13.1g, of which saturates 8.2g; Cholesterol 38mg; Calcium 176mg; Fibre 1.3g; Sodium 79mg.

Mango mania

This rich and creamy shake has a lovely caramel flavour that will appeal to young people and blends brilliantly with fruit purées, especially those made from fruits with an intense, naturally sweet taste like mangoes. It is suitable for anyone following a dairy-free diet since it is made using soya milk, which is particularly good in milkshakes and smoothies.

Makes 2 tall glasses

1 medium mango
300ml/½ pint/1¼ cups soya milk
finely grated rind and juice of 1 lime,
   plus extra rind for garnish
15–30ml/1–2 tbsp clear honey
crushed ice

Cook's tip
If you like very sweet drinks, choose soya milk sweetened with apple juice for this recipe. It is readily available in supermarkets and has a really rich flavour.

1 Using a sharp knife, peel the mango and cut the flesh off the stone (pit). Chop the flesh and put it in a blender or food processor with the soya milk, lime rind and juice and a little honey. Blend until smooth and frothy.

2 Taste the mixture and add more honey, if you like, blending until well mixed. Place some crushed ice in two glasses, then pour over the smoothie. Sprinkle with lime rind and serve.

Mango mania Energy 111kcal/468kJ; Protein 4.9g; Carbohydrate 17.1g, of which sugars 16.9g; Fat 2.6g, of which saturates 0.6g; Cholesterol 0mg; Calcium 29mg; Fibre 2g; Sodium 51mg.

Vanilla snow

This sweet and tasty smoothie will appeal to children, and it is also packed with healthy fruit plus yogurt for calcium and protein. While a good quality vanilla extract is perfectly acceptable for flavouring drinks, a far more aromatic taste will be achieved using a vanilla pod. Its lovely, snowy whiteness is delightfully speckled with tiny black vanilla seeds.

Makes 3 glasses

1 vanilla pod (bean)
25g/1oz/2 tbsp caster (superfine) sugar
3 eating apples
300g/11oz/1⅓ cups natural (plain) yogurt

1 Using the tip of a sharp knife, split open the vanilla pod lengthways. Put it in a small pan with the sugar and 75ml/5 tbsp water. Heat until the sugar dissolves, then boil for 1 minute. Remove from the heat and leave to steep for 10 minutes.

2 Cut the apples into large chunks and push through a juicer, then pour the juice into a large bowl or jug (pitcher).

3 Lift the vanilla pod out of the pan and scrape the tiny black seeds back into the syrup. Pour into the apple juice.

4 Add the yogurt to the bowl or jug and whisk well by hand or with an electric mixer until the smoothie is thick and frothy. Pour into glasses and serve.

Cook's tip
Like most smoothies, this one should ideally be served well chilled. Either use apples and yogurt straight from the refrigerator, or chill briefly before serving. To make a thick, icy version, you could try using frozen yogurt.

Vanilla snow Energy 124kcal/527kJ; Protein 5.4g; Carbohydrate 25.1g, of which sugars 25.1g; Fat 1.1g, of which saturates 0.5g; Cholesterol 1mg; Calcium 198mg; Fibre 1.6g; Sodium 86mg

Simply strawberry

Make this fabulous pink shake for a summer party for girls. Nothing evokes a sense of summer wellbeing more than the scent and flavour of sweet, juicy strawberries. This recipe uses an abundance of these fragrant fruits so, if possible, make it when the season is right.

Makes 2 glasses

400g/14oz/3½ cups strawberries, plus extra
   to decorate
30–45ml/2–3 tbsp icing (confectioners') sugar
200g/7oz/scant 1 cup Greek (US strained
   plain) yogurt
60ml/4 tbsp single (light) cream

Cook's tip
You can replace the strawberries with other fruits if they are not in season. Try using fresh bananas instead to make another very popular milkshake.

1 Hull the strawberries and place them in a blender or food processor with 30ml/2 tbsp of the icing sugar. Blend to a smooth purée, scraping the mixture down from the side of the bowl with a rubber spatula, if necessary.

2 Add the yogurt and cream and blend again until smooth and frothy. Check the sweetness, adding a little more sugar if you find the flavour too sharp. Pour into glasses and serve decorated with extra strawberries.

Simply strawberry Energy 286kcal/1195kJ; Protein 9.1g; Carbohydrate 30.4g, of which sugars 30.4g; Fat 16.2g, of which saturates 8.9g; Cholesterol 17mg; Calcium 217mg; Fibre 2.2g; Sodium 93mg.

Real vanilla milkshake

This deliciously simple milkshake is the cream of the crop and will appeal to the fussiest of children! Nothing beats the flavour achieved by infusing a vanilla pod in the milk beforehand, but if you just cannot wait for the milk to cool, use a teaspoon of good quality vanilla extract.

Makes 2 glasses

1 vanilla pod (bean)
400ml/14fl oz/1⅔ cups full cream (whole) milk
200ml/7fl oz/scant 1 cup single (light) cream
4 scoops vanilla ice cream

1 Using a sharp knife, score the vanilla pod down the centre. Place in a small pan, pour the milk over and bring slowly to the boil.

2 Remove the pan from the heat but leave the pod in the milk. Leave to stand until the milk has cooled.

3 Remove the vanilla pod from the cooled milk and scrape out the seeds with the tip of a knife. Put the seeds in a blender or food processor with the milk and cream. Blend until combined.

4 Add the vanilla ice cream to the mixture and blend well until it is deliciously thick and frothy. Pour the smoothie into two large glasses and serve immediately with stirrers and straws to decorate, if you like.

Cook's tip
This classic milkshake is extremely rich and creamy, but if you'd prefer a lighter consistency, replace half the cream with the same quantity of extra milk.

Real vanilla milkshake Energy 640kcal/2607kJ; Protein 15.8g; Carbohydrate 36.4g, of which sugars 36.3g; Fat 49.6g, of which saturates 30.8g; Cholesterol 83mg; Calcium 475mg; Fibre 0g; Sodium 205mg.

Custard cream float

This fabulously frothy dessert drink makes a wonderful treat that rounds off any meal brilliantly, or you could serve it to your children as a special snack mid-morning or at teatime.

Makes 3 glasses

75g/3oz custard cream biscuits (cookies)
1 large banana
5ml/1 tsp vanilla extract
200ml/7fl oz/scant 1 cup full cream
   (whole) milk
6 scoops vanilla ice cream
banana slices and crumbled biscuit
   (cookie), to decorate
drinking chocolate or cocoa powder
   (unsweetened), for dusting

Cook's tip
For an extra burst of banana flavour, use banana ice cream.

1 Put the custard cream biscuits in a blender or food processor and blend well until finely ground. Break the banana into chunks and add to the ground biscuits. Process thoroughly until a smooth, thick paste forms, scraping down the side of the bowl with a rubber spatula, if necessary.

2 Add the vanilla extract, milk and three scoops of the ice cream and process again until smooth and foamy. Pour into tumblers and top with the remaining scoops of ice cream. Decorate with banana slices and crumbled biscuit and serve dusted with a little drinking chocolate or cocoa powder.

Chocolate nut swirl

Children everywhere will be captivated by this fabulous chocolatey concoction. It is a mixture of melted milk chocolate, chocolate nut spread and creamy milk, marbled together to make an attractive and delicious drink. Adults who like chocolate will love it too.

Makes 2 tall glasses

40g/1½oz/3 tbsp chocolate hazelnut spread
400ml/14fl oz/1⅔ cups full cream
   (whole) milk
90g/3½oz milk chocolate
30ml/2 tbsp extra thick double (heavy)
   cream (optional)
a little crushed ice
2 chocolate flake bars, to serve

Cook's tip
This drink is extremely rich and filling and should probably be reserved for special occasions, but if you feel that using chocolate flakes as novelty stirrers is a bit too much chocolate for your children, serve the drink with multi-coloured straws or plastic stirrers instead.

1 Put the chocolate spread in a small bowl with 10ml/2 tsp of the milk. Stir well until smooth and glossy.

2 Chop the chocolate. Put 100ml/3½fl oz/scant ½ cup of the remaining milk in a small pan and add the chocolate pieces. Heat gently, stirring until the chocolate has dissolved. Remove from the heat and pour into a jug (pitcher). Leave to cool for 10 minutes, then stir in the remaining milk.

3 Using a teaspoon, dot the chocolate hazelnut mixture around the sides of two tall glasses, rotating them so that each glass is randomly streaked with chocolate. Dot the cream around the glasses in the same way, if using.

4 Put a little crushed ice in each glass and pour over the chocolate milk. Serve immediately with flake bar stirrers that can be used to swirl the hazelnut mixture into the chocolate milk.

Custard cream float Energy 485kcal/2027kJ; Protein 9.7g; Carbohydrate 55.7g, of which sugars 41.3g; Fat 26.2g, of which saturates 15.4g; Cholesterol 17mg; Calcium 245mg; Fibre 1g; Sodium 212mg.
Chocolate nut swirl Energy 476kcal/1987kJ; Protein 11.3g; Carbohydrate 46.7g, of which sugars 46.6g; Fat 28.2g, of which saturates 15.3g; Cholesterol 39mg; Calcium 361mg; Fibre 0.5g; Sodium 135mg.

tempting dessert drinks

Irresistible blends that imitate popular desserts are
cleverly transformed into stunning drinks you can
sip leisurely or, in some cases, scoop with a spoon.
Be tempted by true classics such as death by
chocolate and blueberry meringue or, for
something different, try a rhubarb and allspice
cream and an unusual take on banoffee pie.

Frosty fruits

Long after summer is over you can still summon up the glorious flavours of the season by making this fruity and refreshing drink from frozen summer fruits. This purple, slushy, fruity delight will pep up after a hard day at work. Revitalize yourself with this blend and give your body a well-deserved boost.

1 Take the frozen fruits straight from the freezer and put them into a blender or food processor. Blend until finely crushed, scraping down the side of the bowl, if necessary.

2 Add the yogurt and cream to the crushed fruit, then spoon in 00ml/ 2 tbsp of the sugar. Blend again until the mixture is smooth and thick. Taste and add the extra sugar if necessary. Serve immediately, decorated with fruit.

Makes 2–3 glasses

250g/9oz/2 cups frozen summer fruits, plus extra to decorate
200g/7oz/scant 1 cup natural (plain) yogurt
45ml/3 tbsp double (heavy) cream
30–45ml/2–3 tbsp caster (superfine) sugar

Cook's tip
This drink takes only moments to whizz up and you can use any mixture of fruits, whether you've grown your own berries or bought them frozen in bags.

Frosty fruits Energy 174kcal/726kJ; Protein 4.4g; Carbohydrate 20.7g, of which sugars 20.7g; Fat 8.8g, of which saturates 5.3g; Cholesterol 21mg; Calcium 153mg; Fibre 0.9g; Sodium 64mg.

Iced mango lassi

Based on a traditional Indian drink, this is perfect for any occasion: served with spicy food at dinner, at long, hot garden parties, or as a welcome cooler at any time of day. The yogurt ice that forms the basis of this drink is a useful recipe to add to your repertoire because it is much lighter and healthier than classic ice creams.

Makes 3–4 glasses

175g/6oz/scant 1 cup caster (superfine) sugar
150ml/¼ pint/⅔ cup water
2 lemons
500ml/17fl oz/generous 2 cups Greek
    (US strained plain) yogurt
350ml/12fl oz/1½ cups mango juice
ice cubes (optional)
fresh mint sprigs and mango wedges,
    to decorate

1 To make the yogurt ice, put the sugar and water in a pan and heat gently, stirring occasionally, until the sugar has dissolved. Pour the syrup into a jug (pitcher). Leave to cool, then chill until very cold.

2 Grate the rind from the lemons and then squeeze out the juice. Add the rind and juice to the chilled syrup and stir well to mix.

3 Pour the syrup mixture into a shallow freezer container and freeze until thickened. Beat in the yogurt and return to the freezer until the mixture is thick enough to scoop.

4 To serve the drinks, briefly process the mango juice with about ten small scoops of yogurt ice in a blender or food processor until just smooth. Pour equal portions of the mixture into tall glasses or tumblers and add the ice cubes, if using.

5 Top each drink with another scoop of the yogurt ice and decorate with mint sprigs and mango wedges. Serve.

Iced mango lassi Energy 366kcal/1546kJ; Protein 8.8g; Carbohydrate 60.6g, of which sugars 60.3g; Fat 12.9g, of which saturates 6.6g; Cholesterol 0mg; Calcium 221mg; Fibre 2.3g; Sodium 93mg.

Blueberry meringue crumble

Imagine the most appealing flavours of a blueberry meringue dessert – fresh tangy fruit, crisp sugary meringue and plenty of vanilla-scented cream. This drink combines all of these in one delicious milkshake. Iced yogurt is used to provide a slightly lighter note than ice cream, but there's nothing to stop you using ice cream instead for an even greater indulgence.

1 Put the blueberries and sugar in a blender or food processor with 60ml/ 4 tbsp water and blend until smooth, scraping the mixture down from the side once or twice, if necessary.

2 Transfer the purée to a small bowl and rinse out the blender or food processor bowl to get rid of any remaining blueberry juice.

3 Put the iced yogurt, milk and lime juice in the blender and process until thoroughly combined. Add half of the crushed meringues and process again until smooth.

4 Carefully pour alternate layers of the milkshake, blueberry syrup and the remaining crushed meringues into tall glasses, finishing with a few chunky pieces of meringue.

5 Drizzle any remaining blueberry syrup over the tops of the meringues and decorate with a few extra blueberries. Serve immediately.

Makes 3–4 tall glasses

150g/5oz/1¼ cups fresh blueberries, plus extra to decorate
15ml/1 tbsp icing (confectioners') sugar
250ml/8fl oz/1 cup vanilla iced yogurt
200ml/7fl oz/scant 1 cup full cream (whole) milk
30ml/2 tbsp lime juice
75g/3oz meringues, lightly crushed

Cook's tip
The easiest way to crush the meringues is to put them in a plastic bag on a work surface and tap them gently with a rolling pin. Stop tapping the meringues as soon as they have crumbled into little bitesize pieces otherwise you'll just be left with tiny crumbs.

Blueberry meringue crumble Energy 254kcal/1072kJ; Protein 5.6g; Carbohydrate 45.1g, of which sugars 41.5g; Fat 6.9g, of which saturates 3.8g; Cholesterol 11mg; Calcium 151mg; Fibre 0.8g; Sodium 80mg.

Super sorbet fizz

Freshly blended pineapple and cool, tangy lemon sorbet, topped up with sparkling ginger ale, makes a tastebud-tingling, fantastically mouthwatering drink. This semi-frozen blend is perfect after a summer lunch as a light alternative to more conventional desserts, or as a drink that can be whizzed up to allow you to chill out whenever the mood takes you.

Makes 4 glasses

30ml/2 tbsp muscovado (molasses) sugar
15ml/1 tbsp lemon juice
½ pineapple
1 piece preserved stem ginger,
    roughly chopped
200ml/7fl oz/scant 1 cup lemon sorbet,
    slightly softened
wafer thin pineapple and lemon slices,
    to decorate
ginger ale, to serve

3 Add the sorbet and process briefly until smooth. Spoon the muscovado syrup into four tumblers, then pour in the pineapple mixture.

4 Decorate the edge of the glasses with the pineapple and lemon slices. Top up each glass with ginger ale and serve immediately.

Cook's tip

The easiest way to prepare a pineapple is to chop off the top and base, then slice off the skin. Use the tip of a sharp knife to remove the "eyes" and then roughly chop into chunks.

1 Mix the sugar with the lemon juice in a small bowl and leave to stand for about 5 minutes until it turns syrupy.

2 Discard the skin and core from the pineapple and cut the flesh into chunks. Put the chunks in a blender or food processor with the ginger and whizz until smooth, scraping down the side of the bowl once or twice, if necessary.

Super sorbet fizz Energy 126kcal/539kJ; Protein 0.8g; Carbohydrate 32.5g, of which sugars 32.5g; Fat 0.2g, of which saturates 0g; Cholesterol 0mg; Calcium 19mg; Fibre 0.9g; Sodium 11mg.

Rhubarb and allspice cream

Pale shoots of young rhubarb, poached with sugar and spice, and blended with cream, make a truly dreamy concoction. Make this delicious blend early in the season otherwise the rhubarb tastes so acidic that you'll need heaps of sugar to make this the indulgent treat it should be.

2 Transfer the rhubarb and cooking juice to a blender or food processor and process in short bursts until smooth, scraping down the mixture from the side of the bowl, if necessary.

3 Add the cream and milk to the rhubarb purée and blend again until combined. Transfer to a jug (pitcher) and chill until ready to serve.

4 Half-fill glasses with crushed ice, if using, pour over the juice, sprinkle with allspice and serve immediately.

Cook's tip
If you don't have fresh oranges to squeeze for this drink, you can use orange juice from a carton instead, or try a mix of citrus juices.

Makes 4 glasses

500g/1¼lb early rhubarb
100ml/3½fl oz/scant ½ cup freshly squeezed
    orange juice
75g/3oz/scant ½ cup caster (superfine) sugar
2.5ml/½ tsp ground allspice, plus extra
    to decorate
100ml/3½fl oz/scant ½ cup double
    (heavy) cream
200ml/7fl oz/scant 1 cup full cream
    (whole) milk
crushed ice (optional)

1 Trim the rhubarb and cut it into chunks. Put in a pan with the orange juice, sugar and allspice and bring to the boil. Cover and simmer gently for 6–8 minutes until tender. Remove the pan from the heat and leave to cool.

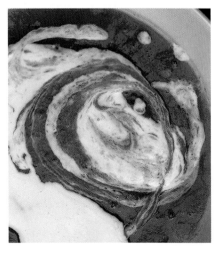

Rhubarb and allspice cream Energy 249kcal/1041kJ; Protein 3.4g; Carbohydrate 25.5g, of which sugars 25.5g; Fat 15.5g, of which saturates 9.6g; Cholesterol 41mg; Calcium 200mg; Fibre 1.8g; Sodium 35mg.

Turkish delight

If you like Turkish delight, you'll love this fabulously indulgent drink. With the scented aroma of rose water and the delicious icy sweetness of vanilla ice cream, it is difficult to imagine a more decadent, or delicious, combination of ingredients.

Makes 3–4 glasses

125g/4¼oz rose-flavoured Turkish delight
475ml/16fl oz/2 cups semi-skimmed
   (low-fat) milk
250ml/8fl oz/1 cup good quality vanilla
   ice cream
a little finely grated plain (semisweet)
   chocolate, or drinking chocolate powder,
   for sprinkling (optional)

Cook's tips

For an even frothier top on this drink, pour the milkshake into a large bowl and whisk with a hand-held electric mixer.

If the Turkish delight is very sticky, you'll find it easier to cut it with scissors instead of a knife.

1 Roughly chop the Turkish delight and reserve a few pieces for decoration. Put the rest in a pan with half the milk. Heat gently until the pieces begin to melt. Remove from the heat and leave to cool.

2 Spoon the Turkish delight mixture into a blender or food processor and add the remaining milk. Process until smooth, then add the ice cream and blend briefly to combine.

3 Pour the smoothie into glasses, top with the reserved Turkish delight and serve immediately, sprinkled with finely grated chocolate or drinking chocolate, if using.

Turkish delight Energy 258kcal/1088kJ; Protein 6.5g; Carbohydrate 42.3g, of which sugars 38.7g; Fat 7.4g, of which saturates 5.1g; Cholesterol 22mg; Calcium 208mg; Fibre 0g; Sodium 98mg.

Banoffee high

Make plenty of this outrageous, lip-smacking milkshake because everyone will love it. Nobody is pretending this is a health drink, but it is guaranteed to give you an energy rush of astronomic proportions. Keep any leftover syrup in the refrigerator to use as a quick and delicious toffee sauce for spooning over ice cream.

1 To make the toffee syrup, put the sugar in a small heavy pan with 75ml/ 5 tbsp water. Heat gently, stirring until the sugar dissolves, then add 45ml/ 3 tbsp of the cream and bring to the boil. Let the syrup simmer for about 4 minutes until thickened. Remove from the heat and leave to cool for about 30 minutes.

2 Peel the bananas, break into pieces and put into a blender or food processor with the milk, vanilla sugar, ice cubes and a further 45ml/3 tbsp of the cream. Blend until smooth and frothy.

3 Pour the remaining cream into a bowl and whip lightly with a whisk or hand-held electric mixer until it just holds its shape.

4 Add half the toffee syrup to the milkshake and blend, then pour into glasses. Drizzle more syrup around the insides of the glasses. Spoon the whipped cream over and drizzle with any remaining syrup. Serve immediately.

Makes 4 tall glasses

75g/3oz/scant ½ cup light muscovado (brown) sugar
150ml/¼ pint/⅔ cup double (heavy) cream
4 large bananas
600ml/1 pint/2½ cups full cream (whole) milk
15ml/1 tbsp vanilla sugar
8 ice cubes

Cook's tips
If you use a blender, read the instructions to check whether it is powerful enough to cope with crushing ice cubes.
   Make the syrup a little in advance so it has time to thicken.

Banoffee high Energy 469kcal/1958kJ; Protein 6.9g; Carbohydrate 54.1g, of which sugars 51.8g; Fat 26.3g, of which saturates 16.4g; Cholesterol 72mg; Calcium 213mg; Fibre 1.1g; Sodium 75mg.

Nutty nougat

For the best results, chill this glorious milkshake for a few hours until it is icy cold and the jumble of ingredients has had time to merge into a hedonistic fusion of flavours. Skinning the pistachio nuts is not essential, but it makes a fabulous visual impact, transforming the specks of nut from a dull green to a gorgeous, vivid emerald colour.

Makes 3 glasses

90ml/6 tbsp sweetened condensed milk
300ml/½ pint/1¼ cups semi-skimmed
  (low-fat) milk
100ml/3½fl oz/scant ½ cup crème fraîche
15ml/1 tbsp lemon juice
25g/1oz/¼ cup skinned pistachio nuts
25g/1oz/¼ cup blanched almonds
25g/1oz/3 tbsp candied peel, finely chopped,
  plus a few extra slices for decoration
ice cubes

2 Add the lemon juice, pistachio nuts, almonds and chopped peel to the blender or food processor and blend until chopped into tiny pieces. Pour over ice cubes in glasses, add a few slices of candied peel and serve.

Cook's tip
Pretty, emerald-green flecks of pistachio nut pepper this rich, nougat-flavoured milkshake, giving it the subtlest hint of colour and the most wonderful texture.

To skin the pistachio nuts, put them in a heatproof bowl, cover with boiling water and leave for about 2 minutes. Drain the nuts and rub them between layers of kitchen paper to loosen the skins. Pick out the nuts, carefully peeling off the remaining skin.

1 Put the condensed milk and the semi-skimmed milk in a blender or food processor. Add the crème fraîche and blend until combined.

Nutty nougat Energy 392kcal/1636kJ; Protein 10g; Carbohydrate 28.3g, of which sugars 27.8g; Fat 27.4g, of which saturates 13g; Cholesterol 54mg; Calcium 266mg; Fibre 1.5g; Sodium 161mg.

Coconut and passion fruit ice

Few things beat the unadulterated, pure flavour of freshly juiced coconut. Whizzed with plenty of crushed ice and teamed with sharp, intensely flavoured passion fruit, it produces a milkshake that tastes indulgently good but is still refreshingly natural and wholesome.

Makes 2–3 tall glasses

1 coconut
75ml/5 tbsp icing (confectioners') sugar
3 passion fruit
150g/5oz crushed ice
60ml/4 tbsp double (heavy) cream

Cook's tip
This tropical, icy, passionately luxurious drink is heavenly on a summer's evening. You don't have to be on holiday to enjoy this type of decadence as this drink can be made quickly and easily at any time. Make a jug full and share with friends or family – if you feel that you are able to share it.

1 Drain the milk from the coconut and put to one side. Break open the coconut, remove the flesh, then pare off the brown skin. Push the coconut pieces through a juicer along with 150ml/¼ pint/⅔ cup water. Stir the icing sugar into the juice and reserve.

2 Halve the passion fruit and scoop the pulp into a small bowl. Set aside.

3 Put the crushed ice in a blender or food processor and blend until slushy. Add the juiced coconut, any drained coconut milk and the cream. Process to just blend the ingredients.

4 Pour the mixture into tall stemmed glasses, then, using a teaspoon, spoon the passion fruit on top of the drink. Add stirrers, if you like, and serve.

Death by chocolate

There are only two ingredients used in this decadently rich smoothie: creamy milk and the best chocolate you can buy. Blended together, they make the frothiest, smoothest and most deliciously chocolatey drink you will ever taste. Once you've tried this recipe, you will never view a chocolate smoothie in the same light again.

Makes 2 large glasses

150g/5oz good quality chocolate
350ml/12fl oz/1½ cups full cream
   (whole) milk
ice cubes
chocolate curls or shavings, to serve

Cook's tip
Depending on personal taste, use dark (bittersweet) chocolate with 70 per cent cocoa solids, or a good quality milk chocolate. If you like the intensity of dark chocolate but the creaminess of milk, try using half of each type.

1 Break the chocolate into pieces and place in a heatproof bowl set over a pan of simmering water, making sure that the bowl does not rest in the water.

2 Add 60ml/4 tbsp of the milk and leave until the chocolate melts, stirring occasionally with a wooden spoon.

3 Remove the bowl from the heat, pour the remaining milk over the chocolate and stir to combine.

4 Pour the mixture into a blender or food processor and blend until frothy. Pour into glasses, add ice and chocolate curls or shavings, then serve.

Coconut and passion fruit ice Energy 247kcal/1041kJ; Protein 1.4g; Carbohydrate 37.1g, of which sugars 37.1g; Fat 11.4g, of which saturates 7.1g; Cholesterol 27mg; Calcium 83mg; Fibre 0.5g; Sodium 229mg.
Death by chocolate Energy 463kcal/1944kJ; Protein 9.7g; Carbohydrate 55.9g, of which sugars 55.2g; Fat 24g, of which saturates 14.5g; Cholesterol 15mg; Calcium 235mg; Fibre 1.9g; Sodium 80mg.

Coffee frappé

This creamy, smooth creation, which is strictly for adults (because of the alcoholic content), makes a wonderful alternative to a dessert on a hot summer's evening – or indeed at any time when you feel you need to indulge yourself. Serve in small glasses or little cappuccino cups for a glamorous touch, and provide your guests with both straws and long-handled spoons to allow them to scoop out every last bit of this delicious drink.

Makes 4 glasses

8 scoops of classic coffee ice cream
90ml/6 tbsp Kahlúa or Tia Maria liqueur
150ml/¼ pint/⅔ cup single (light) cream
1.5ml/¼ tsp ground cinnamon (optional)
crushed ice
ground cinnamon, for sprinkling

Cook's tip
To make a non-alcoholic version of this drink, simply substitute strong black coffee for the Kahlúa or Tia Maria.

1 Put half the coffee ice cream in a food processor or blender. Add the liqueur, then pour in the cream with a little cinnamon, if using, and blend. Scoop the remaining ice cream into four glasses or cappuccino cups.

2 Using a dessertspoon, spoon the coffee cream over the ice cream in each glass, then top with a little crushed ice. Sprinkle the top of each frappé with a little ground cinnamon and serve immediately.

Cool chocolate float

Frothy, chocolatey milkshake and scoops of creamy sweet chocolate and vanilla ice cream are combined here to make the most meltingly delicious drink ever, which is sure to prove a big success with children and adults alike. If you simply adore chocolate and you love ice cream, this may be the perfect drink for you. As this is such a rich, indulgent blend, however, try and resist temptation and don't indulge too often – save it for very special occasions.

Makes 2 tall glasses

115g/4oz plain (semisweet) chocolate, broken
  into pieces
250ml/8fl oz/1 cup semi-skimmed (low-fat) milk
15ml/1 tbsp caster (superfine) sugar
4 large scoops of classic vanilla ice cream
4 large scoops of dark (bittersweet) chocolate
  ice cream
a little lightly whipped cream
grated chocolate or chocolate curls,
  to decorate

Cook's tip
Try substituting banana, coconut or toffee ice cream for the chocolate and vanilla ice cream if you prefer.

1 Put the chocolate in a heavy pan and add the milk and sugar. Heat gently, stirring with a wooden spoon until the chocolate has melted and the mixture is smooth. Leave to cool.

2 Blend the cooled chocolate mixture with half of the ice cream in a blender or food processor.

3 Scoop the remaining ice cream alternately into two tall glasses: vanilla then chocolate. Using a dessertspoon, drizzle the chocolate milk over and around the ice cream in each glass. Top with lightly whipped cream and sprinkle over a little grated chocolate or some chocolate curls to decorate. Serve immediately.

Coffee frappé Energy 489kcal/2049kJ; Protein 8.3g; Carbohydrate 57.6g, of which sugars 55.6g; Fat 23.2g, of which saturates 15g; Cholesterol 73mg; Calcium 255mg; Fibre 0g; Sodium 136mg.
Cool chocolate float Energy 918kcal/3834kJ; Protein 16.9g; Carbohydrate 92.3g, of which sugars 91.5g; Fat 56g, of which saturates 33.7g; Cholesterol 11mg; Calcium 423mg; Fibre 1.5g; Sodium 208mg.

Rum and raisin thick-shake

This rich and creamy milkshake, based on the classic combination of rum and raisins, is remarkably easy to prepare. Use a good quality ice cream, leave it to soften slightly in the refrigerator before scooping, and you simply can't go wrong. If the raisins are a little dry, leave them to soak in the rum for a few minutes to soften and plump up before you blend them.

1 Put the raisins, rum and a little of the milk into a blender or food processor and process for about 1 minute, or until the raisins are finely chopped.

2 Spoon two large scoops of the vanilla ice cream into two tall glasses and put the remaining ice cream and milk into the blender. Process until creamy.

3 Pour the milkshake into glasses and serve immediately with straws and long spoons for scooping up the raisins.

Makes 2 tall glasses

75g/3oz/generous ½ cup raisins
45ml/3 tbsp dark rum
300ml/½ pint/1¼ cups full cream (whole) milk
500ml/17fl oz/2¼ cups good quality vanilla ice cream

Cook's tip
As an alternative, replace the vanilla ice cream with a good quality chocolate-flavoured ice cream – this will taste exceptionally good with rum and raisins.

Rum and raisin thick-shake Energy 789kcal/3288kJ; Protein 15.5g; Carbohydrate 74.8g, of which sugars 74.5g; Fat 43.8g, of which saturates 26.4g; Cholesterol 21mg; Calcium 445mg; Fibre 0.8g; Sodium 237mg.

Espresso crush

A fresh update on iced coffee, this creatively layered treat combines slushy frozen granita with a thick vanilla ice cream layer, and is perfect for rounding off a lazy summer lunch or as a late afternoon refresher. The granita needs several hours in the freezer but will then keep for weeks so it is ready and waiting whenever you fancy a burst of ice-cold espresso.

Makes 4 glasses

75ml/5 tbsp ground espresso coffee
75g/3oz/scant ½ cup caster (superfine) sugar
300g/11oz vanilla ice cream or
    vanilla iced non-dairy dessert
75ml/5 tbsp milk or soya milk

1 Put the coffee in a cafetière (press pot), add 750ml/1¼ pints/3 cups boiling water and leave to infuse for 5 minutes. Plunge the cafetière and pour the coffee into a shallow freezer container. Stir in the sugar until dissolved. Leave to cool completely, then cover and freeze for about 2 hours or until the mixture starts to turn slushy around the edges.

2 Using a fork, break up the ice crystals, stirring them into the centre of the container. Re-freeze until the mixture is slushy around the edges again. Repeat forking and stirring once or twice more until the mixture is completely slushy and there is no liquid remaining. Re-freeze until ready to use.

Cook's tip
The softened ice cream will melt quickly once you start layering it up in the glasses, so a good trick is to thoroughly chill the glasses before using them.

3 Put the ice cream or iced dessert and milk in a blender or food processor and process until thick and smooth. To serve, spoon a little into the base of each glass and sprinkle with a layer of the granita. Repeat layering until the glasses are full. Serve immediately.

Espresso crush Energy 217kcal/915kJ; Protein 3.4g; Carbohydrate 39g, of which sugars 38.3g; Fat 6.3g, of which saturates 4.1g; Cholesterol 21mg; Calcium 115mg; Fibre 0g; Sodium 55mg.

White chocolate and hazelnut cream

This luxurious combination of smooth, creamy white chocolate and crunchy hazelnut is simply irresistible. To get the maximum flavour from the hazelnuts, it is always best to use whole ones, toasting them first to develop their nuttiness and then grinding them fresh, rather than using ready chopped or ground nuts. Add a little nutmeg for a perfect aromatic topping.

Makes 3 glasses

90g/3½oz/scant 1 cup blanched hazelnuts
150g/5oz white chocolate
300ml/½ pint/1¼ cups full cream
 (whole) milk
4 large scoops white chocolate or vanilla
 ice cream
a little freshly grated nutmeg (optional)

1 Roughly chop the hazelnuts using a large, sharp knife, then toast them lightly in a dry frying pan, turning continuously to ensure that they are toasted evenly. Reserve 30ml/2 tbsp for decoration, then put the remainder into a blender or food processor. Blend until very finely ground.

2 Finely chop the chocolate and reserve 30ml/2 tbsp for decoration. Put the remainder in a small, heavy pan with half of the milk and heat very gently until the chocolate has melted thoroughly. Stir until smooth, then pour the chocolate into a bowl. Add the remaining milk, stir and leave to cool.

3 Add the melted chocolate mixture to the blender with the ice cream and a little grated nutmeg, if using. Blend until the mixture is smooth. Pour into glasses and sprinkle with the reserved hazelnuts and chocolate. Grate over a little extra nutmeg, if you like, and serve immediately.

Ice cool coconut

This fabulously cooling, dairy-free drink is just about as silky smooth as they come. Rather than using coconut milk, this recipe opts for desiccated coconut, steeped in water, which is then strained to extract the flavour. Without the nutty texture, this delicious coconut feast slides down very nicely on a summer's evening. If it's the weekend – or even if it's not – and you fancy a bit of a treat, add a splash of Malibu or coconut-flavoured liqueur.

Makes 2–3 glasses

150g/5oz/2½ cups desiccated (dry
 unsweetened shredded) coconut
30ml/2 tbsp lime juice
30ml/2 tbsp icing (confectioners') sugar, plus
 extra for dusting
200g/7oz vanilla iced non-dairy dessert
lime slices, to decorate

Cook's tip
Desiccated coconut can be bought ready sweetened. If using this, you may wish to omit the sugar that's added with the lime juice.

1 Put the coconut in a heatproof bowl and add 600ml/1 pint/2½ cups boiling water. Leave to stand for 30 minutes. Strain the coconut through a sieve (strainer) lined with muslin (cheesecloth) into a bowl, pressing the pulp with a spoon to extract as much juice as possible. Discard the pulp and chill the coconut milk.

2 Pour the coconut milk into a blender or food processor with the lime juice, sugar and non-dairy dessert. Blend thoroughly until completely smooth. Pour into glasses and decorate with lime slices. Lightly dust the lime slices and edges of the glasses with icing sugar and serve immediately.

White chocolate and hazelnut cream Energy 703kcal/2927kJ; Protein 15.1g; Carbohydrate 55.3g, of which sugars 53.6g; Fat 47g, of which saturates 19.2g; Cholesterol 38mg; Calcium 395mg; Fibre 1.9g; Sodium 160mg.
Ice cool coconut Energy 443kcal/1841kJ; Protein 4.9g; Carbohydrate 26.2g, of which sugars 25.7g; Fat 36.2g, of which saturates 29.9g; Cholesterol 5mg; Calcium 65mg; Fibre 6.9g; Sodium 56mg.

fruity
boozy
blends

If you're entertaining friends or simply relaxing
after a hard day's work, try one of these
tasty tipples, which are guaranteed to put
everyone in a mellow mood. Some are fruity and
only mildly alcoholic, while others are spirit-based
and pack a real punch – there's something
here to suit every occasion.

Iced strawberry daiquiri

The classic daiquiri cocktail is named after a village in Cuba that lies near the Bacardi processing plant. The original drink was an incredibly potent blend of rum and whisky but the fruit versions, which are so popular today, are slightly less alcoholic. This one combines sweet and fragrant strawberries with white rum and refreshingly tangy lime juice.

Makes 4 small glasses

4 limes
60ml/4 tbsp icing (confectioners') sugar
200ml/7fl oz/scant 1 cup white rum
275g/10oz/2½ cups strawberries
300g/11oz crushed ice

Cook's tip
To make a really slushy, thick iced daiquiri, use frozen strawberries. There's no need to leave them to thaw, just use them as they are.

To make a banana version of this drink, replace the strawberries with two bananas. Peel the bananas, break them into pieces and add with the rum and icing sugar.

1 Squeeze the limes and pour the juice into a blender or food processor. Add the icing sugar, rum and all but two of the strawberries. Process until really smooth and frothy.

2 Add the crushed ice to the blender or food processor and blend until slushy. Pour the daiquiri into glasses, add a strawberry half to each glass and serve.

Iced strawberry daiquiri Energy 189kcal/789kJ; Protein 0.6g; Carbohydrate 19.8g, of which sugars 19.8g; Fat 0.1g, of which saturates 0g; Cholesterol 0mg; Calcium 19mg; Fibre 0.8g; Sodium 5mg.

Grand marnier fruit punch

The term "punch" comes from the Hindi word *panch* (five), relating to the five ingredients traditionally contained in the drink – alcohol, lemon or lime, tea, sugar and water. The ingredients may have altered somewhat over the years but the best punches still combine a mixture of spirits, flavourings and an innocent top-up of fizz or juice.

Makes about 15 glasses

2 large papayas
4 passion fruit
2 small oranges
300ml/½ pint/1¼ cups freshly squeezed
   orange juice
200ml/7fl oz/scant 1 cup Grand Marnier or
   other orange-flavoured liqueur
8 whole star anise
300g/11oz lychees, peeled
   and pitted
ice cubes
1.5 litres/2½ pints/6¼ cups soda water
   (club soda)

1 Halve the papayas, peel them and discard the seeds. Halve the passion fruit and press the pulp through a sieve (strainer) into a large punch bowl or a pretty serving bowl.

2 Thinly slice the oranges and place them in the punch bowl with the freshly squeezed orange juice, the Grand Marnier or other orange-flavoured liqueur and the star anise.

3 Push the papayas through a juicer, adding 100ml/7 tbsp water to help the pulp through. Juice the lychees. Add the papaya and lychee juices to the bowl.

4 Cover the bowl and chill the fruit punch for at least 1 hour or until ready to serve.

5 Add plenty of ice cubes to the bowl and top up with soda water. Ladle the punch into punch cups or small glasses to serve.

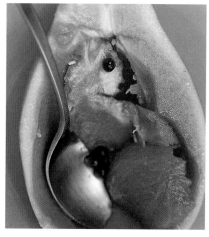

Grand marnier fruit punch Energy 68kcal/284kJ; Protein 0.5g; Carbohydrate 9.3g, of which sugars 9.3g; Fat 0.1g, of which saturates 0g; Cholesterol 0mg; Calcium 15mg; Fibre 1.3g; Sodium 5mg.

Raspberry rendezvous

Pink, raspberry-flavoured bubbles and a suspicion of brandy make this the ultimate in sippable sophistication. A splash of sweet, sugary grenadine added to the jewel-coloured raspberry juice will smooth out any hint of a sharp tang that there might be from slightly underripe fruit.

Makes 6 tall glasses

400g/14oz/2⅓ cups raspberries, plus
   extra, to serve
100ml/3½fl oz/scant ½ cup grenadine
100ml/3½fl oz/scant ½ cup brandy or
   cherry brandy
ice cubes
1 litre/1¾ pints/4 cups ginger ale

Cook's tip
Grenadine is a sweet, ruby-coloured syrup made from pomegranates. It is popularly used to enhance fruit juices and cocktails. True grenadine contains no alcohol, but there are alcoholic versions around.

1 Push handfuls of the raspberries through a juicer and transfer the juice into a jug (pitcher).

2 Stir the grenadine and brandy or cherry brandy into the raspberry juice and chill (preferably overnight, but for at least 1 or 2 hours) until you are ready to serve it.

3 Prepare six tall glasses: add plenty of ice cubes to each and place a few extra raspberries in the bottom of the glasses.

4 Pour the raspberry mixture into each of the prepared glasses and then top up with the ginger ale. Serve the cocktails immediately.

Scent sensation

Orange flower water, which is distilled from the delicate white blooms of the orange tree, gives delicious sweet pear and redcurrant juices a delicate fragrance and a subtle, barely there flavour. Like rose water, it is often associated with Middle Eastern cooking and goes really well with warm-flavoured spices such as cinnamon.

Makes 4–5 glasses

4 pears
300g/11oz/2¾ cups redcurrants
2 cinnamon sticks
45ml/3 tbsp orange flower water
about 25g/1oz/¼ cup icing
   (confectioners') sugar
tonic water
cinnamon sticks and extra redcurrants, to
   decorate (optional)

Cook's tip
If you like, add a splash of alcohol; try an almond liqueur, such as Disaronno, as the almondy edge goes well with the scented flavours.

1 Using a small, sharp knife, cut the pears into chunks of roughly the same size and push the chunks through a juicer with the redcurrants.

2 Crumble the cinnamon sticks, using your fingers, and add to the redcurrant juice. Cover and leave to stand for at least 1 hour.

3 Strain the juice through a sieve into a bowl, then whisk in the orange flower water and a little icing sugar to taste.

4 To serve, put one or two cinnamon sticks in each glass, if using. Pour the juice into glasses, then top up with tonic water and decorate with the extra redcurrants, if you like.

Raspberry rendezvous Energy 122kcal/512kJ; Protein 0.9g; Carbohydrate 15g, of which sugars 15g; Fat 0.2g, of which saturates 0.1g; Cholesterol 0mg; Calcium 18mg; Fibre 1.7g; Sodium 4mg.
Scent sensation Energy 85kcal/359kJ; Protein 0.9g; Carbohydrate 21.2g, of which sugars 21.2g; Fat 0.1g, of which saturates 0g; Cholesterol 0mg; Calcium 52mg; Fibre 4.8g; Sodium 6mg.

Tropical fruit royale

This recipe is a fresh and fruity variation of a kir royale, in which Champagne is poured over crème de cassis. Made with tropical fruits and sparkling wine, this cocktail is a lot less expensive than the Champagne version but still has a wonderfully elegant feel. Remember to blend the fruits ahead of time to give the mango ice cubes time to freeze.

Makes 6 glasses

2 large mangoes
6 passion fruit
sparkling wine

Cook's tip
Delight your guests with this delicious thirst-quencher. With its taste of the tropics, it makes the perfect choice for garden parties on balmy summer evenings, wherever in the world you are.

1 Peel the mangoes, cut the flesh off the stone (pit), then put the flesh in a blender or food processor. Process until smooth, scraping the mixture down from the side of the bowl, if necessary.

2 Fill an ice-cube tray with half of the purée and freeze for 2 hours.

3 Cut six wedges from one or two of the passion fruit and scoop the pulp from the rest of the passion fruit into the remaining mango purée. Process until well blended.

4 Spoon the mixture into six stemmed glasses. Divide the mango ice cubes among the glasses, top up with sparkling wine and add the passion fruit wedges. Serve with stirrers, if you like.

Tropical fruit royale Energy 136kcal/570kJ; Protein 1.2g; Carbohydrate 16.7g, of which sugars 16.5g; Fat 0.2g, of which saturates 0.1g; Cholesterol 0mg; Calcium 21mg; Fibre 2.2g; Sodium 11mg.

Amaretto apricot dream

This really is a dream of a drink, combining fresh, ripe apricots, oranges and delicious maple syrup with creamy cool yogurt. Light and fruity, it is a wonderful choice for a breezy, sunny day in the garden, and the addition of almond liqueur and amaretti gives it a subtle complex flavour. Once you've tasted one you'll surely be back for more.

Makes 4 glasses

3 large oranges
600g/1lb 6oz small fresh apricots
60ml/4 tbsp maple syrup, plus extra
    to serve
50g/2oz amaretti
200g/7oz/scant 1 cup Greek (strained
    plain) yogurt
30ml/2 tbsp amaretto liqueur
mineral water (optional)
ice cubes

1 Grate the rind from one of the oranges and squeeze the juice from all three. Halve and stone (pit) the apricots and put them in a pan. Add the orange juice and rind then heat slowly. Cover with a lid and simmer very gently for 3 minutes or until the apricots are tender. Strain through a sieve (strainer), reserving the juice, and leave to cool completely.

2 Put half the fruit, the strained juice, maple syrup and amaretti in a food processor or blender and blend until smooth. Arrange the remaining fruit halves in the bases of four glasses.

3 Stir the yogurt until smooth and spoon half over the fruits. Add the amaretto, and a little mineral water to the blended mixture (if the juice is too thick), and pour into the glasses. Add the remaining yogurt and one or two ice cubes to each glass. Drizzle with maple syrup to serve.

Cook's tip
To impress guests at parties, use two teaspoons to delicately place a spoonful of yogurt on top of this apricot drink.

Amaretto apricot dream Energy 397kcal/1690kJ; Protein 9.5g; Carbohydrate 86g, of which sugars 80.6g; Fat 3.1g, of which saturates 1g; Cholesterol 1mg; Calcium 227mg; Fibre 9.7g; Sodium 149mg.

Pineapple and coconut rum crush

This thick and slushy tropical cooler is unbelievably rich thanks to the luscious combination of creamy coconut milk and thick cream. The addition of sweet, juicy and slightly tart pineapple, and finely crushed ice, offers a refreshing foil to all this creaminess, making it surprisingly easy to sip your way through several glasses.

1 Trim off the ends from the pineapple, then cut off the skin. Cut away the core and chop the flesh. Put the chopped flesh in a blender or food processor with the lemon juice and whizz until very smooth.

2 Add the coconut milk, cream, rum and 30ml/2 tbsp of the sugar. Blend until thoroughly combined, then taste and add more sugar if necessary. Pack the ice into glasses and pour the drink over. Serve immediately.

Makes 4–5 large glasses

1 pineapple
30ml/2 tbsp lemon juice
200ml/7fl oz/scant 1 cup coconut milk
150ml/¼ pint/⅔ cup double (heavy) cream
200ml/7fl oz/scant 1 cup white rum
30–60ml/2–4 tbsp caster (superfine) sugar
500g/1¼ lb finely crushed ice

Cook's tip

This is a great cocktail for making ahead of time. Blend the drink in advance and chill in a jug (pitcher). Store the crushed ice in the freezer ready for serving as soon as it's required.

Pineapple and coconut rum crush Energy 336kcal/1400kJ; Protein 1.3g; Carbohydrate 24.9g, of which sugars 24.9g; Fat 16.5g, of which saturates 10.1g; Cholesterol 41mg; Calcium 58mg; Fibre 1.9g; Sodium 54mg.

Foaming citrus eggnog

For most of us, eggnog is inextricably associated with the festive season. This version, however, pepped up with orange rind and juice for a lighter, fresher taste, has a much wider appeal. Whether you sip it as a late-night soother, serve it as a wintry dessert or enjoy it as a cosy tipple on a wet afternoon, it's sure to bring a warm, rosy glow to your cheeks.

Makes 2 glasses

2 small oranges
150ml/¼ pint/⅔ cup single (light) cream
plenty of freshly grated nutmeg
2.5ml/½ tsp ground cinnamon
2.5ml/½ tsp cornflour (cornstarch)
2 eggs, separated
30ml/2 tbsp light muscovado (brown) sugar
45ml/3 tbsp brandy
extra nutmeg, for sprinkling (optional)

1 Finely grate the rind from the oranges, then squeeze out the juice and pour it into a jug (pitcher).

2 Put the rind in a small heavy pan with the cream, nutmeg, cinnamon and cornflour. Heat gently over a low heat, stirring frequently until bubbling.

3 Whisk the egg yolks with the sugar, using a handheld whisk.

4 Stir the hot citrus cream mixture into the egg yolks, then return to the pan. Pour in the orange juice and brandy and heat very gently, stirring until slightly thickened.

5 Whisk the egg whites in a large, clean bowl until foamy and light.

6 Strain the cream mixture through a sieve (strainer) into the whisked whites. Stir gently and pour into heatproof punch cups, handled glasses or mugs. Sprinkle over a little extra nutmeg before serving, if you like.

Cook's tip
Note that this recipe contains almost raw egg.

Foaming citrus eggnog Energy 375kcal/1566kJ; Protein 9.1g; Carbohydrate 29.6g, of which sugars 29.6g; Fat 19.9g, of which saturates 10.7g; Cholesterol 232mg; Calcium 112mg; Fibre 0.1g; Sodium 98mg.

index